My Life with
Alexander Archipenko

Frances Archipenko Gray

Frances Archipenko Gray

My Life with
Alexander Archipenko

HIRMER

Contents

Chapter One
The Beginning

As my new teacher opened the door into the small, bright bedroom where I would stay for the summer of 1955, I felt his full scrutiny. Alexander Archipenko was sixty-eight years old, and I was a nineteen-year-old Bennington student on my way to the Yale School of Design. Even though I was shy, however, I wasn't intimidated. I was intrigued. Completely engaged, Archipenko's gaze penetrated even the most mundane subjects: a cracked tree branch scratching at the window, a discolored piece of molding, the worn edges of my suitcase. His attention on every detail seemed to heat up the room.

With a Charlie Chaplin mustache, a paunch, and a bald head surrounded by gray hair, he gave off the unique odor of clean laundry combined with a medley of studio smells. The timbre of his voice was deep, with cadences that traveled from unfamiliar places. Not clearly Russian, Ukrainian, French, or German, his accent was American English with international intonations. His disproportionately large hands were those of

Fig. 1 Woodstock main building, circa 1940s, Archipenko Foundation, Bearsville, NY

a blue-collar laborer. With his clothing and accent, Archipenko would have been out of place in Scarsdale, the suburb of New York where I lived with my parents.

My choice to spend the summer as Archipenko's student before heading off to study with Josef Albers at Yale was one made by default. My instructor at Bennington, of similar but less successful vintage as Archipenko, Simon Moselsio—an academic Russian sculptor who'd studied at the Berlin Royal Academy—had suggested with some hesitation that I might consider Archipenko's school in upstate New York, even though Bennington students had returned with mixed reviews. Another alternative was Hans Hofmann in Provincetown. This was the most popular summer art school for Bennington students, but I was more inclined toward sculpture and Hofmann taught only painting. Also, I'd been to Woodstock and enjoyed the woodsy, casual atmosphere. In choosing Archipenko, my Bennington professor had obliquely warned, I might have a learning experience that wouldn't just be academic or predictable.

My older brother Steve and I certainly couldn't have predicted what we found when he'd driven me to the Archipenko Art School earlier that day. When it came into view through a green canopy of trees at the end of a long private dirt road, the school building (fig. 1) was a surprise. It resembled an abandoned ski chalet. The outside walls of an adjacent structure—containing Archipenko's studio and workshops—were somber, the wood weathered and dark from the creosote that protected it. All the roofs were covered with tar paper, and the main entrance to the school resembled a barn door. Steve commented on the odd rawness of the buildings and was concerned. He felt it was "scary," and my choice to stay was probably very shocking to him. I'd been raised and educated in Manhattan. He'd been a student at Syracuse University and lived in a frat house. This was not a college campus, a summer camp, or even a structured environment, from the looks of it.

Built by Archipenko himself from salvaged materials, the main building was framed inside the damp remains of a stone quarry, a natural fortress with a rock ledge forming part of a wall. The cool interior had a country smell that was mixed with the aroma of Plasticine and moist terra-cotta clay. The cement floor was heavily coated with the same turquoise swimming pool paint that was on the outside balconies, and the furnishings were an eclectic combination of Victorian and farmhouse pieces found at local auctions and secondhand stores. Added to the mix were odd pieces of furniture that were constructed with leftover lumber and paint.

On the second story, where my new room was located, the hallway was actually an enclosed balcony with textured glass windows that hinged at the top and could swing open to the studio below or act as screens. Their purpose, it appeared, was to block dust from rising up from the studio into the living quarters.

Even more surprising to my brother—and to myself—was that I felt no unease with the peeling paint and garage sale clutter. The school, on some thirteen acres in the woods, was worlds apart from my parents' apartment in Scarsdale, where they'd moved from Manhattan four years earlier. They belonged to a country club, played golf, and lived the conservative middle-class life of a second-generation New York Jewish family. Their life in Scarsdale was a prelude to retirement in Florida. They were neither religious nor obviously artistic or intellectual; nor were they particularly ambitious regarding either myself or my brother. However, they had made a great effort to protect me in certain conventional ways and would have been perplexed to learn that taking a shower at my new school could end with a mild electric shock when you turned off the faucet. Lightning storms were hazardous since the grounding was not adequate, and I shall always remember a small bit of lightning traveling through my open hands and down the kitchen sink drain.

My parents wanted nothing more for my brother and me than for us to fit in, to have a decent education, and to follow their model of a comfortable life, which excluded all extremes of ambition or experience. I had no reason not to comply with these expectations until my fateful but innocent decision to study with Archipenko, a decision superficially based on my not wanting to spend another summer in Scarsdale.

As I said goodbye to my brother that day, I also unknowingly parted with a way of life.

After Archipenko showed me how to open and close the glass doors on the second floor—warning me that if I didn't do it correctly, wind or rain might create damage—he hurried off to his next task. His preoccupation felt almost rude, but I was pleased to be treated like someone who could open a window. As I unpacked whatever would fit into the small closet, I mused that even when I was in high school, my father would jump up to raise a window for me, still thinking of me as a child and assuming that I would fall out if I approached the sill. Archipenko, on the other hand, expected competence.

That my bed had a lumpy mattress and still smelled of winter mothballs or that the bathroom I would share with the other students needed a fresh coat of paint didn't matter. The paneled walls of my room were a pleasant faded shade of blue and the door had a glass inset that looked out over the narrow balcony to a large butternut tree—long since gone—where squirrels leaped and blue jays squawked me awake the next morning. The sun was bright and the studio was waiting.

* * *

Four other students and I waited at wooden easels strategically spaced around the room. Before we began working with clay, we were to sketch with charcoal on large newsprint

Fig. 2 Alexander Archipenko, *Mâ Meditation*, 1937, terra-cotta, 52½ x 44 x 17 in. (133.4 x 111.8 x 43.2 cm), Frances Gray Collection

pads, searching for "meaningful forms" by freely drawing one-dimensional shapes. It was Archipenko's idea of creativity in action, which revealed much about his own theories and practice as a sculptor.

Archipenko glanced at each of us in turn. "We don't use models from nature. We don't do naturalistic work. For sculpture, we first draw ideas and then make them in three dimensions." Following nature's way of creating from a seed, he explained, we would then regard the suggestions of an idea in the rough sketch as something to interpret and improvise from—something that would grow to be three-dimensional. This was very different than copying or drawing from nature or a model.

Looking at each of us again, Archipenko added, "I accept only students who are interested in the development of their creative ability." Then he left.

A life-size seated terra-cotta statue of a woman on a pedestal (fig. 2) dominated the studio, and her gaze followed us around the room. Although it wasn't clear whether she was taking it apart or putting it back together, the female figure was casually in charge of a split globe, which rested in one of her hands. I was later to learn that she was the grandest of a series of six statues created from 1933 to 1937 depicting an avatar called *Mâ* in different sizes and poses, with titles such as *Mâ Meditation*, *Mâ Distributing Power*, *Mâ Guiding*, and *Mâ Apparition*.

Under the *Ma*'s stare, the only sounds in the studio were of a stand moving, the scratch of charcoal on paper, and the muffled shuffling of feet on the concrete floor. While casual, the atmosphere was also no-nonsense. There were no soft cushions or comfortably upholstered chairs anywhere, no place to rest except on a high work stool where some of the weight could be shifted off a student's feet.

I had no experience using clay except for making simple pottery at Bennington. Now, working in terra-cotta under Archipenko, I was initiated into the art of sculpture by using this ancient medium. In retrospect, I realize we were not only being shown how to make sculpture, we were also being taught the history of sculpture as a prehistoric human activity. I found it calming to reduce the sculptural complications of human anatomy and to think in simple, expressive forms.

At random times throughout the morning, Archipenko entered to view our progress. The scent of Old Spice mixed with perspiration became discernible as he approached to review our work and help choose the sketch that would eventually be built up in clay. Sometimes he took his hand to a student's drawing to improve a contour, but in Archipenko's classroom there was no chitchat. Although his accent could confuse, when he did speak—even when he expressed ordinary thoughts—his exotic French/Slavic inflection created its own content. Archipenko's deep voice was so arresting that even his silence felt significant.

At the lunch break, as I was heading from the studio to the kitchen, a sliver of tar paper landed on the ground near me, and I discovered what our teacher had been doing while we were sketching. Hanging above me on a ladder that leaned flat against the tar-paper panels of the steeply slanted roof, Archipenko's body was rocking smoothly back and forth in the afternoon sun as he slapped on tar with a spatula. Without his seeing me, I slipped through the door almost directly below him.

After lunch, when we were ready to turn our sketches into sculptures, Archipenko introduced modeling in clay and told us, "Inspiration is the smallest part of creating a work of art. The main ingredients are technical know-how and physical labor." He then taught us to refine our silhouettes three-dimensionally by continually turning the sculpture as we built up volume. Sometimes he encouraged us to get a bird's-eye view to assess if the volumes were balanced in every direction. His approach to creating sculpture at times paralleled the art of cooking, with the quality of preparation and choice of materials equally affecting the end product.

As the early evening sunlight spilled through the windows along with the damp smell of moss, Archipenko arrived for a final review. When he checked my figure, he reduced a contour with a modeling tool and then pressed a piece of clay onto the form with his thumb. He made changes to my work as if it were his own.

* * *

On a short hike to the waterfall behind the school the next afternoon, I came upon Archipenko clearing wet leaves and twigs from around a partially exposed pipe, digging out a narrow channel. He was covered with debris and sweating. As he stopped to gulp some water from a jar, I took a better look at this determined old man. There was something childlike in all this activity, so different from what I expected from grown-ups— at least from those who were in charge, the ones who normally assigned the menial jobs.

When he saw me, he paused, leaning an elbow against the shovel's handle. "The summer's for making repairs. It's good being able to work as a laborer when you have to."

I stared up at the ditch, which stemmed from a weathered hut. Rocks, large and small, moss-covered and barren, dotted the surrounding hillside. A rock ledge crossed over just above where we stood. I noticed outcroppings where wild creatures could nest in tiny cave habitats. Archipenko had planted daylilies, irises, and yuccas to form a carefree garden mulched by smaller rocks and leaves. "What are you digging?" I asked.

Nodding at the small building, Archipenko said, "That's the well house; the pipe that comes down carries the gravity-fed water for the house you're living in." Taking a firm hold on the shovel handle, he went back to removing rocks and leaves. "I empty it for the winter but like to keep it visible so I can tell if and where the pipe has any cracks."

With the help of some of his students, Archipenko had started the construction of the school (fig. 3) in 1940 on a footprint determined by where the stone had been quarried on the side of the hill, known locally as Bee Tree Hill. Locals tracked wild bees for sport, with a tree trunk full of honeycombs the prize. The school building's cement foundation, poured on the rock slab of the quarry, was protected from the inevitable flow of water by several embedded drainpipes that conducted the water from above to under the building and away. The main beam of the house, I've since learned, was probably originally timber for the quarry hoist, and the attic ceiling curved like the inside of a whale or an overturned boat hull. Using technical know-how and principles that worked both mechanically and aesthetically, the entire structure was built with recycled

Fig. 3 Woodstock construction site, 1940, Archipenko Foundation, Bearsville, NY

materials. Secondhand windows and doors were applied to the school building like a collage. The large studio building remained a work in progress, still requiring maintenance and repairs.

I looked at a set of steps a hundred yards away. "Was that a house? I noticed the old plumbing pipes."

Following my eyes, Archipenko picked up his water jar and took a long drink. "That used to be a very nice house I built with all new windows and doors so that my students would have a cozy place to live during the summer. Fortunately no one died when a careless student forgot to turn off the hot water heater a few years ago, but the entire building became an inferno. The local fire squad would only put water on the forest, even though we were all screaming at them. They knew it was too late. Nothing could be saved except the forest." He shook his head and began to dig again. "They still talk about it. Such a waste! No insurance, no house, no replacement. One should only build with secondhand materials. And build it yourself."

Then he smiled. "As you see, I take care of everything."

I would later discover that this acreage was the only land that Alexander ever owned until the 1960s, when he could afford to purchase property in New York City. Financial insecurity was a continuous condition for him, so having land was very meaningful.

As I headed into the woods that day, continuing my hike, the rhythmic scrape of metal on metal faded. I was walking toward the waterfall through a pathway clouded with pale pink mountain laurels (later in the summer I also discovered chanterelles and wild blueberries), the final steep approach hidden behind dense ferns and moss-covered rocks. I felt overheated, and my face was flushed. Here was a way of living that might work for me if I could interpret it appropriately. Self-assurance and saneness of industry made sense. Not that I wanted to shovel dirt or use a pitchfork. But if I had to, I wanted to be able to work with the perseverance and natural dignity I was witnessing. It was contagious, his can-do attitude.

That night I dreamed of meeting a figure in the forest. After walking for a while, we rested together in the moss close by the waterfall, and, looking up through the trees, we were surprised to experience seeing as one person.

* * *

The next day, I stood at the entrance of Archipenko's studio, waiting for him to notice me. The whirling, grinding, and hammering interfered with the calm noises of the forest. It sounded like a factory.

Although he sensed that someone was present, he kept working. This gave me a chance to look around. Nestled against a quarry wall, this woodshed of a studio resembled the entryway to a mine. The barn-style doors hinged to the front part of the studio were wide open, revealing a "Rube Goldberg" selection of pulleys and hoists hung from the ceiling and various grinders powered by an air compressor that was gasping and roaring. Pushed into a dark corner was a half-dismantled brick ceramic kiln, and hanging on the walls and waiting on tables were a large variety of tools, some coated with work grime. Two small windows were blocked by a loft used for storage.

In this dark crowded space was the residue of polishing and grinding all kinds of materials: plastic, aluminum, terra-cotta, marble, and wood. The cement floor had developed a patina, whitened from plaster casting, and the chalky smell complemented the outdoorsy aroma of the earth. Alexander was the owner of all of this activity and alchemy. He had the look of a chef, with his white apron to protect himself from debris and spills.

When he finally acknowledged me, he moved away from the rotating machine. Rather than inviting me in, he came out into the fresh air, a quizzical expression on his face. "Is there anything you need?"

I stared at the worn wood of the barn doors. "Just curious."

With a smile he motioned me in, turned off the air compressor, and showed me the acrylic-glass piece he was completing. Entitled *Spirit*, this sculpture—which today resides in the Norton Simon Museum—would be the last work that he attempted in this medium

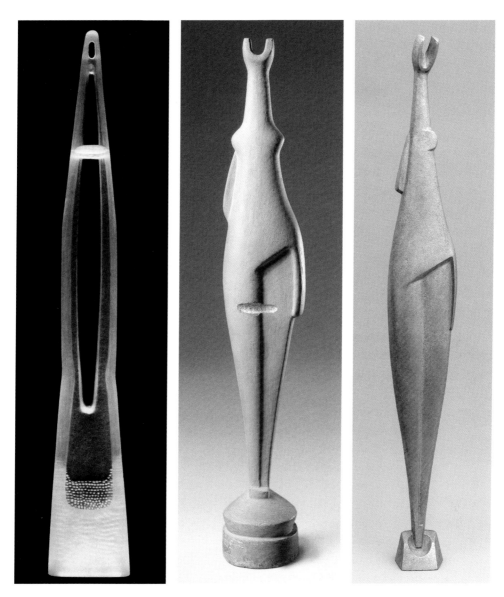

Fig. 4 Alexander Archipenko, *Spirit*, 1956, acrylic glass, electric light source, 46 x 7 x 2 in. (116.8 x 17.8 x 5.1 cm), Norton Simon Museum, Pasadena, CA

Fig. 5 Alexander Archipenko, *Vase Woman*, 1918/19, cast stone, 18 x 3 x 3$^1/_4$ in. (45.7 x 7.6 x 8.3 cm), Hirshhorn Museum and Sculpture Garden, Washington, DC

Fig. 6 Alexander Archipenko, *Vase Woman III (Ray)*, 1956, aluminum, 63$^3/_8$ x 8$^3/_4$ x 6 in. (161 x 22.2 x 15.2 cm), Frances Gray Collection

(fig. 4). His task was to create a surface that would transmit light so that he could sculpt light as a form. Because acrylic glass doesn't refract the way glass or crystal does, he was able to control the visible shape.

Alexander then ushered me into an adjoining studio dedicated to modeling. This inner studio, much cleaner, had been designed and built for privacy. All the windows were above eye level; the working light during the day came from a skylight that tilted north. The painted wooden floor had a slight bounce and a creak, and, after the morning's rain, the smell of the wet earth rose through cracks in the floorboards.

Standing in the center of the room was a plaster of his new work, *Vase Woman III (Ray)*. Over five feet tall, with a smooth surface and streamlined silhouette, it was a new variant and enlargement of an early idea that he'd originally realized in 1918/19 (fig. 5). He had just finished casting it in plaster from Plasticine, a temporary material that in a sculptor's studio represents a form of equity, for it models like clay, never dries out, and can be broken down and used again for other works.

When it was cast in aluminum, *Vase Woman III (Ray)* (fig. 6) would represent Archipenko's transformation of an archaic inspiration in bronze to a modern icon in a contemporary medium, thus embodying a rejection of the old hierarchy of media. Enlarging the original image, *Vase Woman*, to life-size proportions, modernizing the material, and then texturing its surface to make it gently radiant as it absorbs light, he effectively changed the intention of the original work from a vessel into a more engaging presence. An archaic idea of the vase/woman vessel is updated into a streamlined icon that seems about to be thrust into space.

His plan was to exhibit the aluminum *Vase Woman III (Ray)* and several other pieces in this medium for the first time in an exhibition scheduled for the next year at Indiana State Teachers College (now Indiana University of Pennsylvania). Cast aluminum, much lighter in weight than bronze, now felt appropriate for art—in itself it projected contemporary space-age images—and its practicality attracted Alexander.

I took a final glance around. On one wall in the room was an upright piano, and on the other an old rolltop desk covered with handwritten pages. Alexander explained that he was working on a book about his art. I also noticed a bell hanging from one of the rafters. He'd strung a wire from the cottage to his studio so that his wife, Angelica, who had been disabled by a stroke, could signal him. This gave him the freedom to work late or sleep in his studio.

Off this room, tucked into a tiny alcove behind another set of barn doors, I could see the corner of a bed.

As we returned to the main studio, he picked up a small drill which was attached to an air compressor. "Acrylic glass requires a very fine polish so that no scratches are visible unless you want them to make a texture, such as frosting. I built this machine to help me do that." He fixed his eyes on me. "If you want to be an artist, you need to work hard. And if you stop, you die."

* * *

When Alexander paused at my workstand and announced, "You should paint a still life," his deep voice seemed to broadcast through the whole studio, but he was speaking only to me.

Perhaps because he sensed that I wanted to see through his eyes, Alexander had begun to favor me in the classroom, frequently pausing at my workstation to comment. Now, not only would I distance myself from all that red clay, have paint on my hands, and breathe in the different smell of turpentine, but, more importantly, I could advance and receive more individual attention.

I placed my modeling tool on the table. "Okay. What do I need to get started?"

Grabbing a bulky table, Alexander easily moved it to the north wall, under the window. Many of the worktables were constructed from recycled crating materials and painted with odd leftover house paints to freshen them up each season. Because of their vivid colors and simple structure, they looked as if they came from a children's room. With Alexander, nothing went to waste. My table was painted in an orange and turquoise combination—the colors of the Howard Johnson logo. After covering the surface with a sheet of newsprint, Alexander placed a salvaged car windshield on it. "Use this for your palette." He nodded toward the upstairs kitchen. "Now get some objects from the kitchen and assemble them as if they were a painting."

What an easy start. On the newsprint, I randomly organized miscellaneous serving utensils, a red glass bowl, a blue bowl, and a red checkered napkin. As I touched the objects and moved them around, I realized this assignment introduced the intention of constructing in a different way than composing three-dimensional sculpture. This forced me to think about composition more carefully, as every object had its own life of color and volume which needed to interact with the others.

When I stopped fiddling around with the objects, Alexander had a surprise. "Turn around and stop looking at the things on the table. Start to paint what you remember." I wasn't expecting this. I was instructed to not refer to the "actuality," but to invent the equivalent in my painting. Drawing from memory was not my forte.

The assignment was complicated. Looking and remembering. Looking and changing. Alexander encouraged me to use flat planes in order to remember the essentials and to employ a variety of textures to re-create a three-dimensional composition by overlapping flat patterns. The textures and paint were not about creating illusion, but were allusions

Fig. 7 Alexander Archipenko with *Oceanic Madonna*, 1954, Archipenko Foundation, Bearsville, NY

to the remembered object. More than once, I cheated and glanced at my composition.

Then, mixing colors and improvising the organization of the surface became serious fun. The seriousness was in the discovery of an inner logic that was nonverbal. The fun was finally giving in to what was on the canvas and letting it dictate needed changes. I had a new way to see. The surface of the painting demanded its own inner balance and life, and my visual memory began to spin and play within the confines of the canvas. It took a leap of faith, but I had a very good and generous teacher. He taught by jumping right in, taking the brush and messing around in my work—much like a crossword puzzle intruder.

At the same time, Alexander was creating lots of noise and poisonous dust in his studio next door as he used rotating blades and polishing stones powered by an air compressor to cut abalone shell. Previously, in the 1954 work *Oceanic Madonna*, which was now part of a large traveling retrospective through Germany, he had combined abalone shell from the California coast with metal chrome (fig. 7). While abalone shell suggests the sea, nature, and aboriginal cultures, Native American cultures all along the Pacific coast used the shell for decorative purposes and as money. The pieces of cut shell used like mosaic tesserae in *Oceanic Madonna* are employed so differently, in both proportion and purpose, to a traditional church icon that its title referring to a Madonna approaches the surreal. The Formica and chrome suggested synthetic and futuristic civilizations. The combination of natural and man-made materials in this large piece is a symbolic beacon signaling one to a land of universal myth, as well as our present and future commonality. I believe this was Alexander's intent when he created this work. Remnants of the abalone mosaic inspired him that summer to keep cutting more for a later work, *Revolving Figure (The Art of Reflection)* (fig. 21).

When I began studying art, I'd been looking for rules. It's why I'd enrolled at the Yale School of Design. Whatever Alexander was doing, he was clearly not applying or teaching rules and boundaries. Perhaps that was why Simon Moselsio, my Bennington sculpture professor, had reported such mixed reviews from the students who had studied with Archipenko. I had spent an entire semester under Moselsio's tutelage, modeling and casting a female figure without a model, trying to understand the point aside from interpreting a natural form. If self-expression was the result, then I wanted to learn how to do something more—but I wasn't sure what that might be.

Every time Alexander approached my workstation, I felt calmed—even when he picked up a brush and started making changes which forced me to rethink the whole painting. As I worked on my still life, I was convinced that I could learn everything I needed to know from Archipenko. Perhaps the Archipenko Art School was out of the mainstream, yet the ideas to which I was being introduced, although very different from what was then current, were substantial and essentially basic. It was a form of "Modernism" with a twist of appreciation for the organic in nature and the symbolic in the narrative.

When I added palette-knife textures to my painting, the color engaged me differently, producing a static-like resonance. My system had become overcharged, and Archipenko himself was the current that magnetized me.

* * *

As I was leaving the school the next afternoon, Alexander stepped out from his studio next door. "Frances?"

I jumped. He knew my name, but I'd never heard him use it.

Brushing the dust from his hands, he nodded toward the parking lot. "Do you drive?"

"Well, yes, but I only got my license recently." I didn't tell him how recently.

"Good." He led me to an old blue Nash station wagon which he brought out of storage for the summers. "I need a driver."

"I've only driven an automatic." The Nash had standard shift.

Leaning against the hood, he crossed his arms over his chest. "I'll teach you."

I didn't tell him I could use a few lessons. I'd had little time or inclination to practice driving after receiving my driver's license the previous year. A trip down the West Side Highway in my mother's car had ended with a truck driver screaming at me as I exited and ran a stoplight. When it became clear that I was thinking of simply abandoning the car, the policeman who'd been planning to ticket me instead pleaded with me to stop crying and urged me to continue on my way. Then there was the incident in front of my parents' apartment. When I slammed the door after parking the car, the brake released and the car started rolling down the hill toward a four-way intersection. I was able to stop it in time—jumping in and pulling the hand brake—so I never had to tell my mother about it. And I certainly wasn't going to tell Alexander Archipenko.

Although I never found out exactly why his driving privileges had been revoked, it turned out that I was the only one living on the premises who could legally drive the car. After I dashed up the stairs to get my license, I took a breath and slid behind the wheel. The car was neither new nor air-conditioned, but it smelled of summer and I was a little giddy. I was suddenly going to interact with my teacher in a different way. What would we talk about?

Climbing into the passenger seat, he pointed at my feet. "You have to use the clutch to get started in first gear. See how it feels. Use both feet."

As I turned the key in the ignition, the car bucked twice and stalled. When this happened a third time, I could sense that Alexander was also pushing his own feet on

20

the floor. After more grinding and pumping, the car finally coughed into gear.

"Try reverse." Archipenko looked over his shoulder, holding his breath as the car lurched backwards, gravel spitting under the tires. "Good. Let's go."

By the time I shifted into second as we turned onto the main road with its slight hill, I felt the gears stripping. Alexander appeared elated, however. "You made it. Keep going. Just remember to shift down and keep your feet calm. You know how to steer."

It was his confidence that moved the car forward, the same confidence—almost subliminal, a sleight of hand—with which he was approaching me. And I responded. The game was mutual. Even in the simplest things Alexander said and did, I found him magnetic. I caught myself glancing away from the road to sneak looks at him. I wanted to learn everything about him.

The owner of the butcher shop greeted Alexander and cut up a chicken, and Alexander bought the rest of the items he needed for that evening's dinner: a chicken stew for himself and his wife. Our next stop was the vegetable stand, where a very tired-looking dog approached the car and began wagging its tail. When Alexander presented an unwrapped bone, the scene became comical as the arthritic dog, overwhelmed with joy, kept tipping over.

As we returned to the car, I paused. "Perhaps you'd like to drive back? Can't you tell I'm very nervous?"

"You're fine. You'll drive."

Our final stop was the bakery. Addressing "Mr. Archipenko" politely by name, the owner asked after Mrs. Archipenko as she placed the Linzer torte in a pastry box.

By the time we headed home, although the conversation wasn't flowing, I was starting to feel more at ease. It helped that the car was still running. Then Alexander had a new request for me. "Can you type?"

"Yes, but my typing is far from impressive—about on the level of my driving."

"That's good enough." He smiled. "I think you'll like the Linzer torte. Please join Angelica and me at the cottage for tea."

I stared at the macadam road stretching in front of me and realized I was holding my breath.

Chapter Two
His History

Alexander and I walked along the path through the garden, his arms full of the groceries from the backseat and mine holding the pastry box. Red rambling roses and daylilies merged with the local daisies, black-eyed Susans, and Queen Anne's lace wherever the sun was not blocked by pine trees and the shade of the hillside. Juggling the grocery bags, Alexander stopped to select a bouquet from along the path.

After we entered the cottage through a sturdy door that looked as if it had been salvaged from another building, we moved through a gloomy interior, scarcely furnished and hinting of cold winters of neglect—camphor and mold. A bed stood in the sunniest corner of the front room. Simply framed in natural wood, it was crafted well enough to have been worth the voyage from Angelica's family residence in Berlin—her father had been a prominent architect—and then moved from a temporary New York apartment to the summer home in Woodstock. Beside it stood a matching armoire much too large for the modest cottage.

Located at the rear of the building, next to the door leading to the screened porch, were the kitchen and bathroom, narrow parallel rooms, their placement a practical plumbing solution but adding another unattractive touch to cramped country living. The porch, however, was inviting, with the faint murmur of a conversation in progress and the fresh air forcing itself into the silent gloom of the interior space. Upon hearing our footsteps, Mrs. Williams, Angelica's attendant and general housekeeper, came forward and took the packages and the flowers. As she unwrapped them in the kitchen, she cheerfully called to Angelica in a high-pitched Jamaican accent, "Mr. Archipenko has bought us a treat. I'll start the water for a fresh pot of tea."

As we entered the porch, Angelica paused the conversation and greeted me in a cultivated German accent. "It's nice to meet you. Welcome." She was sitting in a wheelchair with one hand cradling the other, both hands finely formed. Her face was slightly lopsided, with her rouged lips drooping a bit to one side from a stroke two years earlier. Thinning hair, carefully arranged, framed her finely complexioned face. I sensed

Fig. 8 Alexander Archipenko, *Angelica*, 1924, lost

the stir of emotion as Alexander and Angelica greeted each other silently—he so mobile, she so anchored. Alexander's arrival was the big moment in her day.

Seated next to Angelica was one of my fellow students, a silver-haired older Swedish woman named Ingeborg Torrup. "Why, hello, Frances," she said. "Come join us."

In their youth, all three had crossed paths in Europe. A successful sculptor from a prestigious German family, Angelica had first met and then married Archipenko in 1921 before they immigrated to the United States in 1923. At about the same time, Ingeborg had been a dancer and actress sponsored by Herwarth Walden, an important entrepreneur of the avant-garde in Germany. Now she supported herself by teaching dance at a Catholic prep school in Tuxedo Park during the winter and spent her summer vacations studying sculpture with Archipenko.

Tea was served on a wooden table looking out on a garden that, in an early spurt of landscaping exuberance, had been terraced and planted with lilacs, tiger lilies, foxgloves, and sweet Williams. A small fishpond that Alexander had constructed and long since abandoned was perhaps more beautiful now for the memory of fish rather than actual ones, which can be a worry to keep alive outdoors. It had rained the night before, and

Fig. 9 Alexander Archipenko, *Angelica's Sarcophagus*, 1925, gold-leafed bronze, 12¹/₈ x 12¹/₈ x 5¹/₄ in. (30.8 x 30.8 x 13.3 cm), Sheldon Museum of Art, Lincoln, NE

the overflow from the small pond streamed down the hill. Everything was overgrown with wisteria, creating the look of a tropical jungle.

As Alexander and I settled into mismatched chairs at the table, the group picked up their conversation again. Angelica had been describing her inordinate fear of thunderstorms. Since she came from the West Indies, Mrs. Williams had a fear of hurricanes. Ingeborg was mostly afraid of ghosts. The conversation continued in this vein for some time, as it amused Angelica to talk about what frightened people. All the better if the fear was incredulous, as in the case of Ingeborg's phantoms.

I had nothing to contribute but curiosity and polite attention. And it was focused on Angelica. Although Archipenko's work had returned to more abstract concerns by the time I met him, many of his works created in the mid-1920s were portraits of Angelica, including one painting, the 1924 *Angelica*, in a Cubist style (fig. 8). Over a dozen pieces have "Angelica" in the title, one of the best known being the 1925 *Angelica* (var. 8), which was re-titled *Angelica's Sarcophagus* in 1959, after her death. This naturalistic horizontal torso, cast in bronze and surfaced in gold leaf, now rests in the Sheldon Museum of Art at the University of Nebraska (fig. 9).

Because Archipenko's main inspiration came from ideas and the exploration of how those ideas might be embodied in form, the implied narrative in *Angelica's Sarcophagus* was just one layer. While the title indicates that the work was inspired by a real person and that person's future resting place, it is also a meditation on the themes of mortality and loss. To project these themes in form, Archipenko experimented with many sculptural innovations for which he became famous, particularly negative space. A missing arm is barely noticed, as it is spontaneously imagined by the viewer, and the arm that is present frames the space behind in a contour that imitates the shape of the figure's eye. However, Archipenko's work can never be reduced to just the material. The body in this sculpture is visibly hollowed out, giving it a shell-like quality, somewhere between a relief and the third dimension. Thus it implies an invisible realm and projects Archipenko's search for the spiritual—the fourth dimension.

Observing Angelica now, I saw that she had the proportions of a large woman, whom I imagined also to be tall. I assumed that she must have been the inspiration for the seated figure in the studio; Archipenko had realized it long before her health deteriorated. Again, however, the *Mâ* series was primarily a vehicle for symbolizing ideas. Even if physically modeled on Angelica, the *Mâ* figure was an imaginary avatar, a mythological super-human being whose job was to lead one into a spiritual dimension. The inscription on the base of the *Mâ* (fig. 2) in the school studio read: "*Mâ* is dedicated to every Mother; to everyone who's in love and suffers from love; to everyone who creates in the arts and in science; to every hero; to everyone who is lost in problems; to everyone who feels and knows eternity and infinity."

Meanwhile, I was finding the real-life Angelica charmingly dramatic. On the topic of fears, she contributed the most compelling story. Arriving in Woodstock by herself early one spring to open the cottage for the season, Angelica forgot she might be afraid at night. "What if a stranger knew I was alone? I had no protection. Then I heard a noise in the woods. I made a bigger noise in the cottage so that whoever was outside would think we were a party of at least four. Then I spoke to myself in a baritone and replied in a soprano. I also tried an alto in French, just to let the stranger know we were an international crowd. We had a wonderful conversation about what to eat for dinner. In a deep voice, I insisted that we have creamed spinach. It was a French meal that I described and on which my 'guests' commented. By the time I set the table and sat down to eat, the uninvited visitor seemed to have gone."

Even half-paralyzed and in a wheelchair, she captivated her audience. Angelica had great style, even in her sadly altered condition. The vignettes of her life that she offered as monologues were always entertaining, her presentation self-assured and flawless. Perhaps because her first husband had been in the theater in Germany, Angelica understood stagecraft.

When the conversation turned to books on religion and philosophy, I remained the outsider, content to listen. Angelica was witty, and at times it was difficult to know what she really believed; she mocked the seriousness of guru followers, yet studied the mechanics of mysticism herself. Gurdjieff and Ouspensky were her favorites.

When Angelica spoke about the inspiration for creating art, a glow lit her face and her eyes were fixed somewhere beyond the porch. "Yes, it's in the subconscious, the famous subconscious, yes. When I start out, I know about what I think I want to do and then it, of course, takes on different shapes, but finally, finally, it always comes back to that vague something which has been the first idea—or hasn't even been an idea yet, but a feeling."[1] She'd been a working sculptor before being hospitalized for high blood pressure and a series of other complaints. In 1953, after several years of poor health, a cerebral hemorrhage had affected her left arm and leg. Now she was hoping to try sculpting again with her one good hand, a goal she would realize the coming winter when she created a small sculpture with two female heads, one listening, the other an abstract figure representing an inner voice. As a memorial on her grave, Archipenko later enlarged the piece and had it cast in bronze.

As Ingeborg talked about the differences between classic and modern art, Angelica became even more animated. "Art is art. There's no difference between classical or modern." Alexander laughed when she added, "There're as many bad paintings in modern art as there are bad paintings in all time in all periods—work that is insignificant and fundamentally not justified. The reason why people hate modern art so much is that they don't understand that all art has the same laws."

Although I wouldn't have ventured to speak, I wanted to ask if she thought Vermeer and Picasso operated by the same laws. Then Ingeborg mentioned Picasso.

Angelica took a sip of her tea. "What Picasso has, of course, one cannot use words to explain it. Except that it's there in every true work of art. The underlying factor is always that great law, just as in biblical times it was the Mosaic law. It's in stone. Picasso has just as much technique as all the old masters, but he's adjusted to our times. The underlying law is there. His work brings up in every person a great curiosity—something that keeps the spirit alive." She wasn't so kind to Salvador Dalí.

Alexander remained attentive, making sure that Angelica had her tea and her sweater. She loved the Linzer torte, which I could see pleased him, for he smiled and responded, "Have more, mon chéri." Throughout the afternoon he would occasionally say something to her privately in French, perhaps asking her which of their acquaintances she'd like him to invite next. As I watched them, I thought how wretched it must have been for her, a woman with a sizable talent who had experienced acclaim as a great beauty in society. Her loss was also his loss. In the past, they'd been what would be described today as a "power couple." As she sadly commented, "My wheelchair will be Alexander's crucifix." I was impressed by his profound loyalty, especially when I later learned that they had lived very separate lives for over thirty years.

When they were young in the 1920s, he'd found Angelica exotic, with her persona of sophisticated decadence. She had the same style and elegance that made Marlene Dietrich and Greta Garbo international movie stars. Even though the physical relationship between Alexander and Angelica had ended long before her stroke, they remained a devoted couple. Their arrangement had evolved into a lasting emotional, intellectual, and domestic bond.

I realized much later that Angelica had probably assumed I'd been invited so Alexander could show me off. She was clearly a woman who wouldn't be jealous; sophisticated and gifted, she didn't have an ego that was tied up with possessiveness. She no doubt presumed I was Alexander's lover. But she was wrong. Even after two years of college, I remained an inexperienced virgin, skittish with men and reluctant to trust boys my own age.

Now, watching Alexander trying to make Angelica happy, I was unconsciously researching what a shared life could be. Their tenderness and respect for each other's past and present touched me. Alexander was a man capable of a depth and emotional intelligence which was new to me.

* * *

I didn't have to knock. The door was open, and Alexander was sitting at his rolltop desk in the inner studio shuffling some handwritten pages. He looked up and acknowledged me with a warm smile. "Please read this and ask if you can't understand my handwriting. Don't worry about mistakes. Someone else is typing the final copy."

It was quiet in this inner studio where Alexander wrote, sketched, and put the final touches on his work. Unless the window was open, we couldn't even hear a car driving up. *Vase Woman III (Ray)* was gone, no doubt to the foundry, and a slight smell of fixative from a pastel drawing being finalized was the only odor.

Once he'd taken the ancient Olivetti typewriter out of its case and deposited it on the desk, I took a seat and started by inserting two sheets of onionskin paper separated by a carbon. When Archipenko sat at the piano and started to improvise, my staccato tapping of the typewriter keys accompanied his singing in a language that I didn't understand. Perhaps a gypsy melody, it was in a minor key and Slavic in spirit.

After about half an hour of struggling with Alexander's handwriting, I was starting to accumulate questions. I hesitated to interrupt his playing, however. The ideas that he expressed were very clear to me, but sometimes the syntax was a little off, and this might change the precision of the meaning. Knowing that what I was doing would serve only as a draft, I kept typing.

The bottle of vodka sitting on a table next to the piano slowly emptied as Alexander poured it into an aluminum tumbler which resembled a large thimble. Finally he pushed himself away from the piano, indicated that I should stop typing, and asked me to join him at the table in another corner of the room. Pouring me some vodka—which I didn't want—into a small glass jelly jar, he began telling me a story about the events leading to his departure for Moscow in 1906 and his move to Paris in 1909.

As he spoke of his childhood in Kiev, I was flooded with a sense of déjà vu, thinking about my maternal grandmother and my paternal grandfather, who both fled Russia. Coincidentally, my grandfather, who was Jewish, fled Kiev at about the same time that Alexander departed. My grandparents never described their early childhoods. This missing link to the past generations of my family history was buried in their despair of having been part of isolated Jewish shtetl communities in Ukraine.

Archipenko, who emerged from a Catholic (Greek) Orthodox Ukrainian background, described his experience as a young art student during the pogroms and political unrest. He and his fellow students, some of whom were probably from Jewish families, rallied against the government brutality, anti-Semitism, and general social constrictions of the times and were eventually expelled from school and threatened with army recruitment—then considered a death sentence.

Alexander talked about the antics of his pet black crow, a thief and trickster with an enormous capacity for loyalty; his peasant background, filled with religion and superstition; the kindness of his grandfather, an icon painter who sat with him while he was healing from an accident and encouraged him to learn to draw; the strict views and discipline of his tyrannical father, who was employed by the University of Kiev with his own mechanical engineering workshop and who opposed his son's pursuit of an artistic career; and the profoundly tender memory of his mother, who was sensitive to art and religion and whose heroic methods had saved him from being an amputee. While he was still a student and living at home, a bicycle crash left him with a severe infection and tuberculosis of the bone. Secretly, away from the vigilance of the family doctor, Alexander's mother found a peasant healer who attended him, brutally cauterizing the wound many times until the infection was healed.

"I was fortunate that my mother refused the doctor's decision to amputate," he told me. When the original attending physician demanded to know how the infection had been healed and to meet the "healer," they were unable to find her. The healer was expecting to be persecuted. At that time, Alexander explained, alternative methods of healing used by the peasant population and administered by "healers" were outlawed by the government.

The healer had burned out the infection with such intensity that although Alexander was cured, he was bedridden for a year. During that time in bed, he pursued art. "I learned to draw because my grandfather brought me books with illustrations of da Vinci and Michelangelo and had me copy them. This entertainment led me to become an artist, and also distracted me from what the family believed would be my future as a cripple."

As he poured us both more vodka, I tried not to look at his legs. He pointed. "That one." I blushed.

"My mother was a very strong person and also very religious. Once I was able to walk with a crutch, she took me on a pilgrimage up the Dnieper River to a shrine. Even though I was still in much pain, I left my crutch behind and walked."

He told this story in a faraway voice, and I wanted to bring him back. "Does your leg ever bother you?"

"I wear a special shoe to support that ankle, and as you can see, I don't limp."

One foot was scarred and slightly lame, but Alexander still had his leg and he'd learned not to complain about pain. Being less than perfect may have increased his pain threshold. It was also clear that his art helped him heal on a deep psychological level. I looked at him more closely. A patina of wear and age enhanced his imperfection. Objects that are weathered have their own beauty.

Without complaining, Archipenko did what he needed to survive—maintaining schools in New York and Woodstock; negotiating with universities and colleges for teaching posts; seeking portrait commissions; managing correspondence, exhibitions, and sales as his own representative; and making his own repairs at the school. He was not your typical elderly man, but a powerhouse of physical and mental determination. And he still found time to be a mentor. When Alexander encouraged me to introduce polychrome on my sculptures (figs. 13, 14), for example, he was sharing an approach with me which was not currently being taught, although it was not new. He led me to new understandings of the universality of art and of form itself.

* * *

By the time the vodka bottle was empty, Alexander's mood had saddened. Perhaps he was mourning his painful relationship with his Russian past, his complex kinship with the Ukrainian émigré community, his youth in Paris, or his volatile connection—usually out of step—with his contemporaries in the arts. This shift in his stature had, in part, inspired his desire to write *Fifty Creative Years*, the manifesto I was typing. Although the text had been developing for some time from his lectures, the book was also an aggressive response to critical attacks on his work. While photographs of his sculptures and slides from his lectures were the core of the book, the text was both his defense and his retaliation, in which he validated the theories and philosophical views that informed his practice.

Op Art, Pop Art, Minimal Art, and Process Art were becoming household words, with the Museum of Modern Art acting as the arbiter of everything new. Even if his work used modern materials, Archipenko was considered passé. Abstraction for the sake of abstraction and the other new trends were outside of his practice if they were exclusive or doctrinaire. In his past he had treated Cubism, Futurism, and Surrealism in a similar manner. Dadaism, which Archipenko came to avoid and disdain, may have led to his detour away from the New York School of the fifties and sixties.

At the same time, he was also the author of his own problems. Much of his estrangement from the contemporary art world had surfaced in April 1944, when he alienated himself from the Museum of Modern Art and its director, Alfred Barr. Issues connected to Archipenko's participation in the 1936 MoMA show *Cubism and Abstract Art* set off a decade of acrimonious correspondence between the two men. The friction began with a misunderstanding, and Archipenko had some responsibility for its prolongation and intensity. Two distinct issues which continue to haunt Archipenko's reputation today—antedating and replication—were at the heart of the conflict.

Katherine Jánszky Michaelsen astutely outlines the background and chronology of the dispute in her 1986 essay for the exhibition *Alexander Archipenko: A Centennial Tribute*. As she explains, the sparring began over a date.[2] When Barr questioned the 1909 date Archipenko had assigned to *Hero* (fig. 10), Alexander changed the date to 1910, but the tone of his letters implies his concession was mixed with resentment that Barr had the power to question the dating.

The more pressing yet ancillary issue was replication. Having explained that the works Barr requested for the show were in European collections and therefore unavailable, Archipenko sent replicas,

Fig. 10 Alexander Archipenko, *Hero*, 1910, plaster or bronze, 18 in. (45.7 cm), location unknown

Fig. 11 Alexander Archipenko, *Boxing*,
1914/1935, terra-cotta, 30¹/₈ in. (76.6 cm),
Peggy Guggenheim Collection, Venice, Italy

not originals. Archipenko had no problem justifying this decision in his accompanying
note to Barr:

> I am sure that by now my work has already arrived in New York. From these
> works only the "Sculpture-Painting" is the only one existing original example.
> The others are the replicas of the old statues. . . . Those which I have sent you
> are also originals because every one was sculpted individually and was not
> produced from a mold.[3]

Although Alexander had cleaned the slate with this note, Michaelsen suggests that
"Archipenko's information about the replicas either did not register with Barr, or he chose
not to act on it."[4] It's easy to speculate that Barr may have felt duped and trapped into a
deception that did not allow him to turn back.

It is, however, Barr's opinion of Archipenko's non-Cubist works that must have been
most painful for Alexander to absorb and probably created his desire for the bloodbath
that followed. As Michaelsen explains, although Barr acknowledges Archipenko's
achievements, he "singles out *Boxing* (figs. 11,12) as Archipenko's 'most abstract work
and most powerful' and comments that it has no trace of the 'mannered prettiness' of
the later work."[5]

Fig. 12 Alexander Archipenko, *Boxing*, 1914, plaster, 23³/₄ x 16⁵/₈ x 16 in. (60.3 x 42.2 x 40.6 cm), Solomon R. Guggenheim Museum, New York, NY

Stepping back in time, I can imagine the impact Alfred Barr—being only thirty-four years old and the first director of the Museum of Modern Art since its opening five years earlier—had in publishing this destructive comment. It is difficult to imagine that Barr was blind to the effect such a public remark would have. It was an unnecessary cruelty.

The warm welcome given to Jacques Lipchitz by Barr and the rest of the art establishment in New York in 1941, Michaelsen suggests, also "seems to have upset Archipenko."[6]

In 1944, the conflict came to a head over questions about the antedating of two terra-cotta figures that appeared in the 1936 show. When Barr reproached Alexander for having exhibited replicas with inaccurate earlier dates in the MoMA show, Alexander's tone became much more shrill. At the end of a long and irate letter addressed to Barr, Alexander wrote:

> At the present moment and as a final reply to you I should say, that it is with pain and indignation that I write to you this message: After spending 20 years in this city, I finally am confronted with your desire to study my art, and if 20 years were not enough for you and the Museum of Modern art [sic] to learn the exact truth about my work then please don't interfere now and please keep your hands off my art.[7]

While there were some with a profound respect for Archipenko's artistic contribution who cheered him on, he never came back into fashion following this battle with Barr. Even though it failed to materialize, at the time of the conflict there were artists, critics, and collectors waiting to get Archipenko's manifesto titled *That Is Why I Request to Remove My Art from the Museum of Modern Art*, for which he was sending out announcements. But realistically, no artist of the time could afford to oppose the power of the New York art world. Both James Soby and Barr tried to appease Alexander, but their efforts failed to bring about a full reconciliation. Prophetically, many of the questions raised in this conflict—specifically antedating and replicas—would color the rest of his career.

Once it was clear Archipenko was at a stalemate with the powers at MoMA, the best he could do was to ignore the whole episode, continue working—which he did—and turn his efforts back to Europe. In 1949, he arranged for an exhibition of his prewar plasters at the Galerie im Rathaus Tempelhof, the municipal gallery in Berlin. The show was organized by Professor Erich Wiese, who later became head of the Hessisches Landesmuseum in Darmstadt. Perhaps not fully informed of the MoMA disaster, Wiese had only memories of another Archipenko from before the war, a generous friend who had trusted him and sent him packages of food and clothing when he and his family were in need. The plasters for the show had been stored since 1923 in the Berlin studio of Carlo Pott, a stone carver and fabricator who had worked for Archipenko before the war.

During the summer of 1955, when I met him, Archipenko was still directing his energies to Europe. His hopes for public encouragement and economic relief were with his retrospective exhibition traveling in Germany. Just before packing up to come to Woodstock, he'd crated and shipped from New York all the work for this show. Acting as his own representative, Archipenko had scheduled the exhibition to tour six German cities, starting in Darmstadt. This required long rounds of correspondence between Archipenko and his new dealer, Herr Klihm. For the German tour, he took sole charge of the correspondence, photography, and general follow-up details. Today, such a project—even with the convenience of the Internet and digital images—would be handled by a large staff. Alexander had spent his own money casting the bronzes and even built the crates himself, but there were still bills from the shippers that he'd neglected to pay.

After four years of the extensive costs associated with Angelica's hospitalizations and most recently her stroke, Alexander was stripped of cash. Sometimes bartering sculptures for medical care, he used all his contacts—former students, collectors, friends of friends, and social services—to cobble together the bare resources for his wife's medical care, which included hiring an air ambulance to transport her from Duke Hospital in North Carolina to Mount Sinai Hospital in New York. Barely able to pay his rent in New York or keep up his mortgage payments on the Woodstock property, he was using commercial foundries to save costs when I met him.

As I tucked the typewriter back in its case that night and agreed to return the next evening, I mused that if Alexander had a totem it would be a bull. His body charged into action, and he always seemed to have the stamina he needed, whether it was to complete a sculpting experiment, patch the roof, or attend to students.

That night, after a long day which included many hours editing every surface of my new piece, I dreamed that my body took on the shape of my sculpture and I was moving naturally within its form.

Chapter Three
Intimacy

Alexander dropped a stack of two-by-fours on the ground between us. "I have a project for you. But first you must build the table on which to do it."

I stared at the wood, its edges stubbled with splinters. As he came back with a grimy tool chest, Alexander smiled. "And I'll help you."

The extra attention with polychrome painting had given me confidence. Now I was graduating to new experiments and skills—wood carving and multi-material reliefs. This was a gift. The knowledge that my teacher was testing me with the very problems that absorbed him that summer instilled in me a sense of self-value as a creative person.

My first wood carving, *Muse*, was a two-foot high polychromed statuette hand-carved from a piece of mahogany (fig. 13). It was conceived first as a drawing and needed a specific size of wood. To that end, several pieces of mahogany were glued together, and I used carving tools, rasps, files, and emery cloth to disguise the joinery. Alexander showed me how to sharpen my tools. The physical challenge of carving and constructing large works made me feel accomplished.

On another occasion, I carved the wood first and then glued the carved contours together to look like a solid shape in wood, creating the three-dimensional *Aphrodite* (fig. 14). Then, to symbolize regeneration, I engraved an image of the sculpture on the figure's "belly." The carving and the name were inspired by an ancient icon. As with *Muse*, I began with a drawing.

For my first bas-relief, *Primeval*, I started with a sketch which I enlarged on wrapping paper and then tacked down to a piece of mahogany (fig. 15). At the lumber yard, the owner cut out the outlines with a jigsaw and glued the forms together with clamps. Then I fastened the two-dimensional carvings to a flat surface. For me, the piece suggested a flower coming from the sea, the early genesis of something prehistoric. Against the dark background and rough texture of scratched black paint with white paint showing through, I painted part of the relief a fiery red. For *Turkish Statue* (fig. 16), I turned to a more whimsical theme, seeking more contrast in color. It has brightly colored shapes that suggest the look of pantaloons.

The experience was total immersion as I learned how to carve, build things, use a drill, make templates, and focus on a project and see it through.

In the fifties, a lack of competence was assumed to be part of feminine appeal, part of the "Barbie doll syndrome," and my family unconsciously encouraged me to believe that my aspirations should be limited, or at least sexually appealing. At the time, marriage and family were the primary goals for young women of my background, and women married young—usually directly after college. If being a middle-class wife and mother in a family like mine was to be my destiny, though, I wasn't quite sure why I was taking up space. Why would I want to create more of the same? And I was a misfit. Still frightened by the male aggression I perceived in boys my age, femininity felt like living the life of an animal stalked through the woods.

The summer after high school, in 1953, my mother took me on a trip to Paris and London, where friends of friends had age-appropriate sons. To prepare for our European trip, she imagined me styled as something between Audrey Hepburn and Grace Kelly. Without understanding that the more attractive I was, the more endangered I felt, she

Fig. 13 Frances Gray, *Muse*, 1955, wood, 25 in. (63.5 cm), Frances Gray Collection
Fig. 14 Frances Gray, *Aphrodite*, 1955, wood, 24 in. (61 cm), Frances Gray Collection

insisted that my hair be streaked blond for the trip. My eyes stung from the smell of the peroxide. The entire procedure was torturous—an initiation ceremony almost as awful as the contact lens ordeal, which I was unable to tolerate. Even though I was very nearsighted, Mother made it quite clear that wearing glasses was as bad as being flat-chested, and she encouraged me to wear eye makeup and take my glasses off at all times. She also brought home a selection of panty girdles, padded bras, and crinolines.

Her failed attempts to socialize me started on board the ship and continued throughout Europe. In Paris, she arranged for me to meet a family friend's son, a medical student attempting to learn French before his studies began. As a courtesy, he escorted me around the student quarters in Paris and took me to a garden party. I was interested in Paris, not him.

In retrospect, I realize my mother was attempting to give me all that she had craved and not received at my age. She was her definition of a generous and loving mother. While I know her hope to improve me as a general upgrade from her life was natural and well-meaning, it made me quite unhappy, angry, confused, and eager to leave home for college.

When I arrived for the summer at the Archipenko Art School after two years at Bennington, I still hadn't had a real boyfriend. Sexually, I was ready to find out more, but there was no one whom I trusted—or who trusted me, for that matter. Now, as I worked with carving tools, color, and texture to create my sculptures, life was magical. When I observed the world that surrounded me, it looked new and alive. I didn't want to be someone's wife. I wanted to be an artist in a paint-stained shirt with clay dust in my hair.

A dedication to art would dominate every decision I made, and Alexander provided the rationale. I was coming to think of him as something Old Testament—on the order of Moses parting the Red Sea. Whether or not it was practical or normal, it had a perfect inner logic for me. The fullness of a life that rejects fear and embraces newness and experimentation was a compelling model.

Before I was even aware of it, his fearlessness and self-mastery were attracting me to him in a deep and profound way. It was these thoughts, in part, that would hurl me into an uncharted world, one anchored to Alexander Archipenko and his life.

* * *

The evening was following its usual pattern. Alexander had just come down from the cottage, having settled Angelica for the evening, and I'd watched the light go on in his studio from the window of my bedroom. It was twilight and the scent of wild spearmint drifted from the ground as I followed the path behind the school. If the few students still eating noticed me passing by the kitchen window, I was unaware of it.

The door was left open for me, as it had been for the past week, and Alexander was sitting at his rolltop desk arranging the typewritten pages from the day before. "These are good, Frances." He handed me the new handwritten set. "Just keep doing as you've kindly been doing."

After Alexander ended a Slavic song on the piano and I'd managed to finish several pages, exchanging typos for grammar improvements and spelling corrections, he motioned for me to stop. "Would you like some vodka and some kielbasa sausage that my Ukrainian visitors brought me? It's very good. Have some. I'll read the typed pages tomorrow."

It was now after nine o'clock, and he'd finished off more than one tumbler of vodka. As I returned the French/English dictionary to the shelf where he also kept tattered art books, I stopped to read the titles. Appearing beside me, Alexander removed two books from the shelf and handed me one. "You can borrow the Bergson book for as long as you like. You should know what he says about art: 'More and better.'" Participating in life, seeking "more and better," was Henri Bergson's dictum, and Alexander had lived by it since his early twenties. He was still living by that slogan when I, now almost twenty years old, met him.

"Come sit down. Let's look at the Greek sculpture book together." Alexander brought the book to the worktable, where he'd set up the vodka tumblers and two plates. Once he'd poured me some vodka, which I really didn't want, he sliced me some sausage, which I did. I was hungry—and also very curious about what he would say about ancient sculpture.

Opening the well-thumbed and tattered book, he flipped to a set of illustrations. "Look at these archaic sculptures. They were the beginning. Let me tell you about them."

I noticed these pages were the most worn—the ones showing the female figures.

"These are the original earth goddesses. Sometimes they were only play dolls that symbolized fertility." Alexander stopped to slice us more sausage. "In Kiev, when I was a child, lying on the ground near my house was a huge stone earth goddess named *Nana* that dated to prehistoric times. Every day I passed her on my way to school. I discovered other fertility goddesses later, when I went to the Ethnographic Museum in Paris. They seem to appear in all sizes and many variations all over the world."

I was familiar with most of the photographs from my art history courses in high school, but reviewing the works in this new context—not as history, but as sculpture—I now studied the profound simplification of these primitive little figurines. They projected enormous power, having many of the same attributes as Mayan clay figures, and looking at them, I experienced something visceral that bridges time and culture. It was the kind of instant connection that is described as an epiphany.

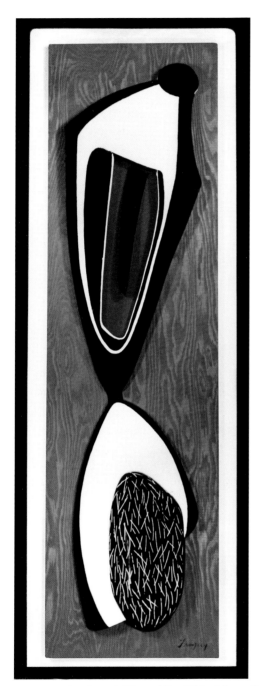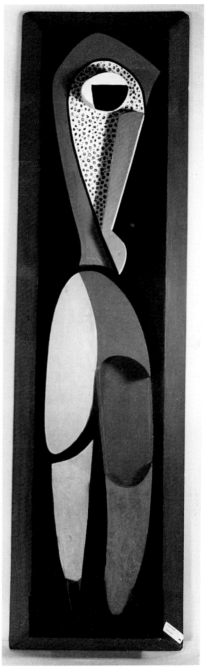

Fig. 15 Frances Gray, *Primeval*, 1955, wood, 48 in. (121.9 cm), Frances Gray Collection
Fig. 16 Frances Gray, *Turkish Statue*, 1955, wood, 48 in. (121.9 cm), Frances Gray Collection

Taking a long drink, Alexander placed his cup on the table. "Ancient people signal to us from the past with these sculptures. We're all connected by universal symbols."

What Alexander had to say seemed profoundly important to me, both when I read his words while typing them and when I listened to him talk. I wanted to be closer to him and to know him better. Soon I found myself keenly aware of the pleasant country mustiness, the carelessness of rusty nails tossed about, and the carefulness of sharpened tools. Alexander's voice was taking on texture. He was a wonderful storyteller—and, as I was about to discover, a very sensitive lover.

He didn't have to seduce me. He wasn't exactly what I was expecting, but when I met Alexander, I was ready. Even though he had a reputation with women and I'd seen him flirting, Alexander was also the first man I felt safe with. Uncomfortable with any hint of male aggression, I found myself relaxed with a mature, tender, and respectful lover. There wasn't any reason to say no out of fear or embarrassment.

Sex in the fifties had a lot of tags attached to it. Girls could easily be labeled, shamed, and otherwise tortured. Boys had their own set of concerns. What was often missing was a healthy sense of humor and someone with experience to lighten the burden. My father was strangely informative. "All women are the same when you turn them upside down." From my mother's perspective, I was supposed to save my virginity for my husband. It was a precious gem. Getting married was certainly not something I planned to prepare for by remaining a virgin. In Mother's view, however, I didn't have much else to offer, since I was flat-chested and wore glasses, and her attempts to help me improve had failed. Oblivious to the contradiction, she also declared I would never know who a man was until I "slept with him" and gave up this irreplaceable jewel.

Alexander demystified sex for me. There was no exchange of precious jewels. And this was indeed a good way to get to know him, as Mother had advised. He was experienced and discreet. Just as his extraordinary regard for women is reflected in his famous sculptures of female torsos, Alexander adored women's bodies. He loved giving a woman pleasure. He took his time. After making love, he wrote a message with his index finger on my back. Then he told me a story and asked me to tell one too.

In the studio with Alexander, outside noises were muted and the world itself at a far distance. The smell of untreated wood from the walls that bordered the bed mingled with a domestic aroma from the soap in the adjoining tiny bathroom. It was all so easy that Alexander thought I was much more experienced than I was.

This was how I wanted to live. I suspect that I also hoped on a subliminal level that becoming lovers would tie him more closely to me.

While on the surface it would have been easy to assume the cliché—I was a vulnerable young girl seduced by a charismatic international artist and my teacher—

Alexander and I were forming what I knew wasn't a traditional relationship. Many boundaries were broken. That he was my first lover, that he was almost fifty years older, and that he was married to an invalid wife whom he loved deeply seemed complicating—if not impossible—obstacles to our forming a bonded relationship. Yet we did. I had been a person out of touch with my body. In spite of the fact that our ages were all wrong and our backgrounds even more at odds, Alexander made me feel beautiful, loved, even smart.

Back in my bedroom drifting off to sleep that night, listening to the persistent rattle of the beechnut tree branch against the window, I reminded myself to be careful. My reality could slip. It had happened before.

* * *

My mother's alarmed voice on the phone to my father broke into my daydreams as I sat at the vinyl-covered kitchen table with milk and butter cookies, watching the pigeons on the fire escape. It was the summer I was fourteen.

My mother's voice went up an octave. "You have to come now. My brothers are monsters. They're bringing my father here to see my mother!"

I stopped dunking my cookie. What? My dead grandfather was alive?

As my mother had always told the story, her father, the gambling black sheep son of a rabbi from Albany, abandoned my grandmother and left her penniless. My mother then became a bookkeeper and the sole source of support for her mother, who assumed the role of widow when they moved from Albany to Los Angeles to create a better life. "I had it easier than my mother did and I really had nothing to complain about," my mother told us. That her older brothers had by this time gone their separate ways and left my mother with full responsibility for their mother didn't upset her. "That's how boys are."

But apparently my grandfather wasn't granted the same immunity—and my grandmother wasn't a widow.

My mother was hysterical. "Please come home. You have to stop this." Because my missing grandfather was ill, now, after almost twenty years, my uncles were bringing him to see the wife he'd abandoned. Mother began shouting into the phone. "I don't want him anywhere near our apartment or near me and my family. I don't care if he is sick!"

I dropped my half-eaten cookie. What else did I not know? Since I was young, I'd had the recurring daydream that my life was just a film role and I was just an actress. Fantasizing that life in my home with this family was one among an endless number of changing roles and films was my escape from a household where reality was elusive—distorted by "white lies."

When I was a very young child, on the rare occasions when I disobeyed my mother, she always responded with the same threat: "Wait until your father gets home!" My punishment was her anger and a long day filled with the fear of an unknown reaction from my father. Upon his arrival home from work, she'd announce my father's assignment. "You have to punish Frances. She was impossible today!"

His hands on my shoulders, gently steadying me, he would lead me into my room, close the door, place me on his lap, hug me, kiss my cheek, and instruct me to scream. "Really scream and cry as loud as you can so Mommy thinks I am doing a good job." He'd turn the incident into a private joke.

To add to the confusion, because he was absent from the house during the war years, he had become a stranger to me. Yet I was expected to love this person just because he was my father and the breadwinner. For me, reality became shifting and amorphous, and in my fantasies, no one had a permanent identity. Invisible parallel universes existed in my mind. Now, two weeks away from returning to high school, I learned that a real parallel universe existed in my family. Discovering this secret confirmed that I was an outsider, not protected, shut out.

I felt myself fragmenting into pieces, yet ventured from the apartment building. Outside, the world was suddenly hyper-sensory. Buildings seemed charged with electricity, and—like the colors I had been painting during the summer—they looked more and more luminous. On the streets, people appeared shadowy and ominous. When I crossed through the park at 178th Street, I was sure my grandfather was there spying on me from the raised terrace where my grandmother used to sit sunning herself and talking to neighbors. Strangers who passed me seemed to have identities that had significance, if I could only figure them out.

What I could not do was explain my shifting reality—which I later learned was dissociation—to my parents. When my father demanded, "Frances, talk to me!" I remember responding as if in a stupor, "I'm too sleepy to talk." His cigar smoke was suffocating.

"Okay, Frances, we're going to a doctor. You must stop crying and acting strange! If you don't stop this, you won't be able to go back to school." A week or two had gone by. Determination evident in her straight, unbending posture, my mother was dressed to go out in her suit and navy blue high-heeled pumps, hat on, gloves in hand, and with a splash of Chanel No. 5 dabbed behind her ears. Just before grabbing her matching purse and the keys, she checked that I was presentable, which meant that I was wearing a panty girdle and stockings.

Through our family doctor, she'd arranged to have a psychiatrist evaluate me. As we walked together up the block to Fort Washington Avenue to hail a taxi, the world started to shift slightly back to where it had been before everything became different.

When we arrived at the office, I was ushered into a dimly lit library with a clumsy oversized desk. After motioning me to sit opposite him with the desk between us, the psychiatrist asked me a series of questions in a very calm voice. As I remember, they were very simple and impersonal—neither challenging nor prying. Although this session was supposed to be an evaluation, it became therapeutic. After that appointment and a follow-up one a week later, I was no longer dissociating and was ready to return to school.

Even though I heard nothing more about my missing grandfather, I never forgot the feeling of walking next to the edge and having the sense that my reality was tentative. Being in the company of my family usually reinforced this sensation.

* * *

When my mother arrived at the Woodstock school that summer, she rolled her eyes at my sweatshirt smeared with clay and paint. She was still disappointed that I wasn't continuing to streak my hair. On the other hand, the fact that I was studying with a famous European artist was some compensation. Perhaps it signaled a step toward an interesting future.

As I showed my mother and the friend who had accompanied her around the school, my mother brushed at the imagined dust settling on her shoulders. She and her friend were both dressed for the country, my mother in her suburban mode of a crisp white camp shirt tucked into a pair of seersucker culottes, a white cashmere cardigan draped over her shoulders, and a gold charm bracelet dangling from her wrist, her large diamond engagement ring a bit too dazzling. Her short-cropped gray hair, earrings which didn't dangle, and matching blue espadrilles and canvas purse all said "country club."

I ushered my guests back into the sunshine as soon as possible and onto the hilly path to Angelica's cottage, where we'd been invited for tea.

On the way my mother repeated for her friend a story I knew well. "When I was young, my mother wouldn't let me pursue a career in Hollywood, even though I'd been invited more than once to take a screen test." Mother shook her head sadly. "She believed being an actress was bad form and that it was more respectable to be a garment district bookkeeper with modeling duties."

Well, my mother could certainly act. As she entered the porch of the cottage, her face flushed from the walk up the hill on this warm summer day, her smile was pure showbiz. But I knew better. I felt her awkwardness mounting as my mother—who craved stability and order—eyed the porch's screens, which were dotted with rips and clogged in spots with lint. For all she knew, spiders had crawled over the table and insects had shared the sugar bowl earlier in the day. Cleanliness and high polish were my mother's expectations for a tea party.

Angelica's smile radiated across the rough surface of the table with an expression slightly askew, her carmine lipstick exaggerating the asymmetry of a once-perfect face. "Please come in and sit down. It's a pleasure to meet you." Angelica edged the wheelchair slightly back from the table. As always, one hand gripped the other until she loosened her good hand and held it out to my mother.

When my mother shook Angelica's hand and slid into a mismatched wicker chair, her own smile was exaggerated. The disabled made her uncomfortable. I knew also that she was slyly observing the frayed napkins and the oversized monogrammed German silver. The silver was real, but not a matching set, and it was polished from use rather than by a maid. The slightly sardonic tone that came with Angelica's cultivated German accent also increased my mother's wariness.

I heard a drill switch on in the distance as the kettle started to boil in the kitchen. I wanted to be in the studio. Anywhere but here. While I melted into my chair, I was reassured by Angelica's sophistication and her ability to appreciate without judgment people from a different background—which now included my mother.

It was Angelica who moved the conversation along. As a good hostess, she first sought out common ground. When she learned they'd driven from Scarsdale, she volunteered a story about her time as a patient at the Burke Relief Foundation, a rehabilitation center in Westchester County, where I coincidentally had done volunteer work during one of my nonresident terms at Bennington. "My daily routine at Burke was an endless round of social activities. Although I would have been happy by myself, they scheduled me for bingo and crafts with the other patients." Angelica paused for effect. "Perhaps it was my fault, because when I was interviewed, I had been left waiting for the psychologist for a long time. When he finally arrived, he asked me why I was looking through the telephone book. I told him I was lonely and wanted to see how many people I knew. He must have been responsible for planning my daily routine."

My mother laughed, but glanced at her friend.

My mother's friend volunteered that they both played golf.

"Ah." Angelica nodded. "Yes, I can see you both have very strong arms."

When my mother's friend flexed her muscles, everyone laughed—except me.

That afternoon, Alexander stayed in the background, and I imagined that Angelica was covering for us. Although she never gave me any overt indication, I intuited that she knew everything—and enjoyed the knowledge.

It was beyond my mother's imagination, of course, to consider that there was anything going on between my teacher and me. Waving a cheery goodbye in the parking lot, she had no complaints about my becoming an artist, and the fact that I would be entering the Yale School of Design in the fall made up for my glasses and lack of a hairdo.

Meanwhile, my nightly routine with Alexander had grown comfortable, and once my initial jumpiness subsided and curiosity took over, there was much to learn. When we were able to spend time alone together, I felt protected in the tiny, den-like room, filled with the double bed covered in an Indian textile bedspread.

Although I was aware of Angelica's bell, I don't remember ever hearing it ring when Alexander and I were together. But then, I posed no threat to her. Alexander never left her side if she had a bad day or asked him to remain with her in the evening. Angelica and Alexander came as a pair. I was content to be on the sidelines of their lives.

When they met, she was a known artist in Germany and they were of the same generation. He was already an international figure, but Angelica's elevated social status—she was a famous society beauty, a member of the Dresden Secessionists, and, more importantly, had a father who was a prominent architect—evened things out. In essence they were balanced partners. When she died, I knew he'd be stunned. I thought of them as swans that mated for life.

I was from a different bird species altogether. With me he sought another kind of experience, one that followed a pattern. I was the last in a list of creative women whom he nurtured and at times simply played with. Although his relationships often connected through mentorship, I recognized his disinterest in domination. Attracted to women who had the ambition to pursue an artistic career, he also wanted an equal partner, even if he had to build that person up to the task. This was definitely my case.

In turn, I believe that Alexander experienced female companionship as a source of renewal. He had idealized Angelica, and he idealized me, but in a different way. Our connection was more like a Trilby story, but without his development into a full-blown Svengali or my disintegration. There was a transformative process going on, and I was the project in development. He hoped I would achieve success as an artist at the same age that he had.

Alexander saw himself as clear water, a medium through which a higher awareness rippled. Although he was not without self-interest, his commitment to his art sought a moral purpose by reflecting universal truths and laws. For him, the artist was merely a conduit for this elevated consciousness. I would repeat his early history—the fame and glory of being discovered as a young genius, a new conduit. The vitality of youth was my magnet.

* * *

As Alexander and I drove home from dropping off the final accumulation of typewritten pages to the editor/typist, he announced a surprise. "Okay, Frances, you have some really nice small sculptures in Plasticine. I want you to pick one or two of your pieces in plaster to be cast at the foundry. Then I'll show you how to do the finishing. We should get them back in time for us to experiment with patinas before the end of summer."

I started to cry. Alexander was alarmed. "Do you want to stop the car? Are you all right to drive?"

I composed myself and continued driving. This type of generosity and faith in my abilities was so new to me. I didn't know how to tell Alexander that was the reason I was crying. I hadn't believed my good fortune when he had encouraged me to work in polychrome and wood. Now he was offering to take me further. Living with my family just four months earlier, I'd been given to believe that if I opened a window I'd fall out.

The next morning Alexander helped me build the armatures and cut the metal gates, something that was technical and a bit tricky. Then he stood over me as the plaster I'd mixed in a white enamel bowl hardened into a warm, unusable mass. This would be the first of many times that I would go through this process. Even plaster needs to be mastered, and I hadn't appreciated how quickly it sets. The initial preparation in all its stages must be done correctly, and, as I found out, it was very easy to ruin the whole thing. Alexander patiently guided me, step by step, through one failed attempt after another. "Just throw the plaster out and mix less the next time. Not so thick. You're getting the knack."

The morning felt precious, the air fresh and poignant with the hint of summer's end. The wild grass was drying out and seeds were forming. As squirrels jumped from branch to branch on the tree above us, occasionally a butternut would thud to the ground.

When Fred Aurori, the metal caster who managed the Sheidow Foundry in Farmingdale, Long Island, arrived with his wife, I was ready with two plasters. One was going to be cast in aluminum and the other in bronze. Fred had trouble relaxing, and his wife was very concerned about him. "He only has half his stomach left," she told me in a private aside as the men went into the studio to settle over vodka.

The foundry where Fred was taking our pieces used the sand casting technique, a system perfect for casting bronze that had a smooth surface and few undercuts. At that time most art foundries used the lost-wax method, a process that was longer and more expensive.

That night as I looked at Archipenko's back while he played the piano, I felt like crying again. During the first summer of our relationship, there were so many things absorbing him. All these years later, I'm still amazed that he found the time to include me in his life in such a harmonious way. I know he cared about me, but he also cared about Angelica, his school, the show in Germany, his book, the water pipes, and, before everything else, making time to work undisturbed in his studio.

Artistic geniuses like Archipenko have more power of will than most. I imagined him as having the qualities of an Olympic athlete. I remembered his words: "If you stop, you die."

There was little more than a week left before the summer ended. Although the weather was still warm, the roses were long gone and all that remained were the hips and thorns, hidden by the leaves. Wild daisies still appeared, but the forest sounds were beginning to change. As the sun started to orbit lower to the earth, the intensity of the green landscape was softer in the twilight.

Without admitting it to myself, I had become attached. To be the lover of the Twentieth-Century Modernist Sculptor Alexander Archipenko was to be with a complex and fascinating personality—creative genius, confident self-promoter, devoted husband, sensitive lover, generous and demanding teacher, spiritual seeker, arrogant iconoclast, charming host, urbane Ukrainian, and vodka drinker.

I had no interest in finding a different or younger man, nor the desire for a partner or sole companion. My attitude toward Alexander was not based on being loyal to one person or behaving in a prudent way for the sake of being good or bad. I felt a unique bond growing. However, the summer had been its own entity, with no references to the future.

As the day neared that Alexander and Angelica would return to New York City and I would leave for Scarsdale and then Yale, I felt myself dissociating. A perceptible glow began to attach to the objects around me and the visual world became fantastic, filled with color, texture, light, and shapes.

I had walked close to the edge, and I was beginning to slip.

Chapter Four
My One-Person Cult

When I entered Josef Albers's tight little office, having been singled out by the class monitor for discipline, Albers didn't ask me to sit. "Do you have a problem? I'm told you're causing one." He looked straight at me with neither menace nor benevolence, very self-contained.

I met his stare. What had the monitor reported?

Before spending the past summer with Archipenko, I'd been looking forward to studying at Yale, stepping up to a change from Bennington's predominantly female population and bucolic landscape and into a more disciplined institutional setting. And at first, it felt empowering to be one of a sprinkling of female students in a sea of men. In a room of sixty males in the Albers color theory course, we five women were guided to seats reserved for us in the front row. But this soon became tedious as we "girls" felt targeted by adjunct teachers and male monitors, one of whom pressed me to pose for his photography project.

Even more irritating was Albers's program of color theory, a required class. Although it was catalogued as his course, Albers never appeared. Instead, the class was taught by adjuncts and supervised by monitors who took their authority with a ludicrous amount of self-importance. So much of what was being taken very seriously I found to be self-evident and dry. "Color" was the last thing that I was experiencing. The prepackaged colored papers that we were given to "play with" and prove the theory made it worse. Even more disturbing was the daily warm-up drill—like calisthenics—meant to demonstrate the difference between horizontal and vertical lines. We were expected to move our arms to indicate that we really "got" this.

In the "design is science" academic formality at the Yale School of Design, the message was pervasive: when you're in school, you're not an artist, you're a student. I'd already learned this when I discovered I was too low in the pecking order to use empty studio space outside of class.

Finally, after six weeks of what I found to be a robotic and demeaning class, I acted out my dissatisfaction by not raising my arm. When challenged by one of the monitors, I met his glare and spoke calmly. "Although I understand what you want us to do, I would like to have an explanation for why I should do it."

The monitor took this personally, just as he had taken my rejection to pose for his fashion photography project. He motioned for me to follow him from the class. Everyone else was okay with the curriculum and thrilled to be there as a student. Obviously, I was not getting the point. Now that I found myself in Josef Albers's office being told I was causing a problem, I attempted what I thought to be good manners. "Mr. Albers, it's a great honor to meet you at last. I would like to have an explanation for why we are expected to move our arms vertically and horizontally in unison in every color theory lecture." While Archipenko believed I was already on my way to being an artist, at Yale I was merely a student—which meant a nonentity—who had overstepped the bounds and was worthy of neither studio space nor an opinion. The Archipenko Art School had spoiled me; Alexander was in my head, taking my part.

The color in Albers's face deepened as he rose from his chair. "Why are you here at all? This is not the place for you." He placed his hands on the desk and thrust the upper part of his body forward, as if about to launch himself at me. "You must leave the school, and none of your tuition will be refunded."

I was startled at the sudden emotion from this self-contained man. There must have been a bit of irony in my tone that caused his reaction. I'd rattled him. I surprised myself as I backed toward the door. "Actually, I'll tell my parents not to complete the payment."

I called my mother, told her to stop the check, and packed. The Yale School of Design, it was clear, had been a mere interruption in my connection to Archipenko and the work that interested me. I had yet to contact Alexander, however. My nervousness to do so puzzled me. Although it had been evident that he would welcome me as a student at his New York school, I hadn't called or written him while I was at Yale. One part of me assumed—knowing his ability to compartmentalize—that when I was out of his sight, I was out of his mind. I also believed there was little I had to offer. That I missed him on a personal level wasn't an emotion I was ready to examine too closely. Much clearer to me was my role as his protégé.

When I reached him, Alexander made it all so simple. "Please come as soon as you're ready. The school is open—you can start at any time."

Telling my parents that I intended to commute from Scarsdale and continue my studies with Archipenko in Manhattan received no argument. What choice did they have? For now, they were thankful that I had a place I wanted to be. After all, I was only nineteen. And I was a female, so they had no great expectations. In fact, being kicked out of Yale interrupted the only career path my parents had imagined for me. And it wasn't artist. My job had been to find a husband.

In preparation the previous spring, my paternal grandfather had told my mother, "Take Frances to the furrier. She's ready for a fur coat." If you had an extended second-generation New York family which had successfully adapted to the upper middle class, you typically had a furrier in the same way you had a dentist, doctor, or lawyer. The coat was part of the package for going on the market. In the fur district, where my new coat would be stored until wintertime, I was measured and fitted with a canvas template, and then my nutria fur coat was made to order. Properly groomed as a Jewish Grace Kelly, I was ready to go to New Haven and find the right match.

Now the coat was hanging unused at the furrier's and I was about to attend art school in a seedy neighborhood in New York City, one with presumably no eligible mates.

* * *

After hurrying through the entrance to the building, which was a haven for derelicts—warm, enclosed, and unattended—a slow, rickety manned elevator brought me to the second floor. Alexander hadn't yet arrived, so I sat near the door with my back against the wall in the dimly lit hallway, clutching the lunch bag that my mother had packed. That morning, my father had driven me down the bumpy West Side Highway and dropped me off at the Archipenko Art School at Broadway and 66th Street.

Located in the once-famous Lincoln Arcade Building, Alexander's school was in a labyrinth of studios that occupied the entire block and would later be torn down to become the footprint of Lincoln Center. In its prime, the Lincoln Arcade was home to artists ranging from George Bellows to Marcel Duchamp, as well as dancers, musicians, and eccentrics. Now most of its tenants were residents left over from a better era, and the smell of neglect and booze permeated the neighborhood.

By the time Alexander arrived, I must have fallen asleep.

"Are you okay?" His deep voice was gentle. "You can't sleep here. Come on. Get up." He was standing there, smiling, unchanged, happy to see me. Absorbing the sparkle in his eyes, my fears dissolved.

As his hand found my elbow, Alexander led me through a narrow, windowless, tomb-like corridor lined with crates and sculptures to a cramped and makeshift set of rooms where everything seemed haphazardly placed, ready to be either packed or unpacked. In a tiny space partitioned off with a cot and a hot plate, Alexander made me coffee in his Italian coffeemaker while four students—whose tuition paid the rent—wandered past us to the main room.

In the large space where Alexander worked and taught, street light filtered through a wall of dusty windows that looked down onto the traffic island on 66th Street, where local derelicts sat on benches and enjoyed the sun. It was the familiar smells that told me the New York studio was Alexander's home base. Newly opened packets of plastiline filled the studio with a spicy smell like cardamom, as did the slightly toxic aroma of turpentine and shellac. Then the damp smell of plaster curing cleansed it all, a bit like the whiff of rain on pavement. Alexander's favorite tools rested in assorted metal boxes next to a stack of crates in which they'd be packed for the return trip to Woodstock the following spring. He was very good about keeping all his running wheels oiled in machine-shop fashion, and, as in Woodstock, the focal point in his New York studio was the noisy air compressor that animated whatever tool or rotating wheel he was using. The atmosphere in the studio felt like an organic whole, informal and fluid. I felt in place.

In the "office"—a long table with a chair in the windowless hallway—Alexander officially registered me and asked me to continue doing his typing in exchange for tuition. The old typewriter from Woodstock was waiting.

I agreed, but there seemed to be very little space for students. The sculptures in the studio—the ones that were visible—were not easily approached since nothing was arranged for viewing, and covered workstands were pushed to one corner. Most of the stands in use were Alexander's. In his apron with his sleeves rolled up, he was rotating his attention between several sculptures at the same time as he continued work on the exhibition for the spring of 1956 at Indiana State Teachers College.

While I watched him, it wasn't possible to distinguish where the energy and motion began or ended. This was his studio, his universe spinning with rotating tools and abrasive sounds. Never stressed, Alexander maintained an athlete's posture, and there was no separation between him, the tool, and his sculpture. When he worked, his knife, spatula, or jigsaw became an extension of his body. Watching him explained why live concerts are popular. We want to watch the musician move the instrument—not just hear the music.

He didn't talk. He saved theory for formal lectures and occasionally the students working in a section of the room.

It was clear that one lonely bust waiting for attention on a worktable didn't require any theory. This was business, not art—a commissioned portrait of the Ukrainian industrialist William Dzus. With the ongoing distress about Angelica's illness and the cost of her care, Alexander was less inspired to do his own new work in the fall of 1955 and was rather courting and completing portraits and other commissions. The life-size bust of Dzus would be cast twice, for placement in two of his factories. Inventor of the quarter-turn fastener—a screw essential for motor engines, which modernized airplanes and continues to be used in racing cars—Dzus was part of the Ukrainian community that Alexander could tap to get some cash flowing. Of the same generation and diaspora experience, Archipenko and Dzus also had similar raging-bull demeanors. They differed in that Dzus was unbelievably rich through his inventive genius, and Alexander was extremely broke despite his. Dzus had made billions of dollars from one screw.

Alexander's connection with Ukrainians had a long history, beginning when he first arrived in Paris in 1908/09. Considered a national hero in later years, he appreciated Ukrainian patrons encouraging their friends and relatives to collect his work. A frequent visitor during those days was Dr. Wolodymyr Wozniak, who purchased sculptures and ultimately helped finance the publication of Alexander's book, *Fifty Creative Years*. Alexander executed many works related to Ukrainian culture—including four separate portrait commissions of the national poet, Taras Shevchenko—some of them for the Ukrainian Institute of America founded by Dzus. To celebrate his Ukrainian heritage and support its culture, Dzus used his earnings to found the institute in a mansion he purchased on Fifth Avenue's Museum Row. I glanced at the unfinished portrait. Dzus was not a handsome man.

By afternoon, the Dzus bust was covered like a canary in a cage, and Alexander was building a crate for the traveling exhibit in Germany. The screeching of his jigsaw blocked out all other sounds. Completely absorbed with several of my own plaster models in progress, I barely registered it when the studio fell quiet again. There was adequate Plasticine for me—like Alexander—to work on more than one sculpture at a time, and by early afternoon, I already knew the day would not be long enough.

I did notice, however, when an old girlfriend who was now Alexander's occasional secretary stopped by to help him out with correspondence. She was also expecting to stay, and he had to calmly coax her out of the door at four o'clock in the afternoon. I thought what a heartbreaker he must have been in his heyday.

On a hot plate in his makeshift kitchen, Alexander made me a very highly-seasoned chicken cacciatore for dinner. Earlier in the day, when he'd looked at what I unpacked for lunch, he'd walked me down Broadway to buy a cut-up chicken from the butcher. "You can't live on carrot sticks and a boiled egg. You're too thin. We will have one of my picnics after work tonight."

After hours and away from the expected, the outside world disappeared and we were alone in the private back room of his studio. We told each other stories and enjoyed an intimacy that for me defined romantic adventure. We were like children together. Yale was a dim memory.

* * *

Amidst the hurly-burly of Canal Street with its grime and discards, Alexander rummaged in the corners and through the bins of a shop that sold used tools and odd pieces of plastic and metal remnants. His use of color was often dependent upon the color of the artificial or natural material he was working with, whether that was a sheet of Bakelite or abalone shells. One factor in Alexander's creativity during this period came from his inclination to recycle. He also made constructions using hardware, hinges, and fasteners. He didn't like to throw out workable things or parts. He gave engines that were no longer in use to the mechanic down the road, who in turn would give Alexander a hand if he needed to retool an engine or find a part.

When I spotted some tiny glass tiles in different shades of blue, I knew I could use them. The tiles were left over from some job, probably dumped off by a contractor to gain a few bucks on the sly. As Alexander negotiated with the owner in the gloomy rear of the shop, I instinctively moved away to tables on the sunny street, where various dusty wrenches, screwdrivers, and emery cloths were displayed. This section of New York merges in my memory with the Lincoln Arcade Building: bright light dissipating into cave-like somberness, unshaven derelicts, and the smell of traffic and street food vendors. Manhattan toxicity at its best. Alexander and I mined the place for ideas as well as materials.

That morning my father had dropped me off at the train station, where I'd joined a male friend my age for the trip to Manhattan. Still hoping that I would meet an appropriate young man and get married, my parents were pleased that I spent Saturdays traveling to Manhattan with their friend's son. This was a ruse that covered both his activities and mine. Until my "date" and I met to return home on the same train at night, neither of us knew what the other was up to. Nor did we ask.

My family still had no idea that my relationship with Alexander was anything but that of teacher and student. It was beyond my parents' powers of imagination that I would be having an affair with a man the same age as my grandfather, especially one who wasn't well-groomed. It wasn't just the age difference. The Broadway studio was a world very much apart from where I was raised. At least my brother had followed the rules I was disregarding. He married at the age of twenty-one, directly after graduating from college, went into the army for two years, and then worked for my father. Before long, he had two children. The Lincoln Arcade, where I spent so much of my time, smelled of poverty and had all the connotations that my parents spent their lives avoiding.

But Scarsdale was a dead end for me. A small room next to the kitchen, originally meant for a maid or an infant, was where I lived until I figured out how to leave permanently. Staying with my father's parents overnight in Manhattan didn't alleviate my trapped feeling. The little room in Scarsdale was also my last connection with my maternal grandmother. For a brief semester break while I was still at Bennington, I served my grandmother—bringing her tea and sitting next to her in the same way she had tended me through all my childhood illnesses. While I stayed in the little room, my grandmother slept in the larger second bedroom, which was decorated like a television den with two single beds or "studio couches" against the walls; it denied being a real bedroom. It was "for the sleep-over guests" who never came, just as the maid's room never housed a maid—only me, an unmarried child waiting for a life. But I'd found one. I looked at the box of blue glass in my hand. I had a life devoted to art, with a mentor who believed in me. Encouraged by Alexander's improvisations and recycling which resulted in amazing new works, I felt set free to use my imagination and take my own risks. Later that morning, I found a dusty piece of lead sheet from which I could assemble an interesting bas-relief.

When Alexander and I weren't browsing in and out of his favorite shops on Canal Street on Saturdays, we went uptown to look at the fabrics at the Spanish Museum or rambled through the Museum of Natural History, viewing fish and fauna in camouflage, Native American totem poles, and all the sundry rocks and gems. We ignored the labels; they got in the way of looking.

Although we spent more time in the Museum of Natural History and hardware stores than the Metropolitan Museum of Art, Alexander also gave me advice on how to learn from the work in an art museum. His approach was technical. He was interested in how other artists had solved problems. You decided what element you needed to know about—perhaps how a surface might be treated—and then wandered through the museum on a random hike, looking at only that element in a series of great masterworks or minor works. He didn't differentiate between a Rembrandt or a Grandma Moses. He was interested in what the artist was doing. Was the surface shiny? Did it absorb or reflect light? It was a very random process. The only thing not random was your initial focus.

In sculpture you might be looking at texture or at how different materials did different things. Wandering among Greek archaic sculptures, we might notice simplified shapes that were similar to what Brancusi did later, which came from a universal need to simplify. In Egyptian art we would follow

Fig. 17 Alexander Archipenko, *Flat Torso*, 1914, bronze, 15¼ x 4⅝ x 4⅝ in. (38.7 x 11.8 x 11.8 cm), Frances Gray Collection

the line in work that was flattened out, not three-dimensional. I wondered if that was where Alexander derived the idea for his *Flat Torso* (fig. 17). In Asiatic art there was always a great deal of symmetry, which got lost in Western art during the Renaissance. Symmetry and silhouette were important to Alexander, and he could trace their significance in Asian art. Another exercise he encouraged was to look at what was considered a great masterwork and approach it as if you were the artist and needed to decide if there should be any changes.

All this activity away from the studio increased my energy and imagination. Alexander encouraged a playfulness that assumed some risk taking. It was irresistible. During the rest of the week we fell into a routine. I commuted from Scarsdale and was busy in the studio for at least eight hours, either typing or turning my ideas into plaster models to be cast in metal. Most nights, after we'd spent a few hours alone, Alexander walked with me to Grand Central Station and saw me off on the eight o'clock train home. Then he returned to Angelica, who was in their apartment on 19th Street with a caretaker.

I was only somewhat aware of his ongoing distress about Angelica's progressing illness. It wasn't that Alexander was private about what was going on in the rest of his life. It was just that he was only where he was when he was there. His ability to compartmentalize his activities gave stability to our relationship, and I followed his example. I too was living a double life. In part, I confess, it was the secrecy I found exciting. For me, secrecy was emotionally interchangeable with escape.

Was it love? It didn't matter what it was. When Alexander superimposed his experience and seriousness of purpose on me, I was a "goner." It was a bit of brainwashing on his part, and I was in a one-person cult. The twinkle in the blue eyes under his very serious brow made it happen for me. He moved mentally and physically as one all-powerful, magical being.

* * *

It was December 1955, and my trip from Scarsdale in the early morning had been cold and dark. As I had every day for the past three months, I arrived at the studio well before nine o'clock. Today, however, I had to wait outside because Alexander didn't hear the bell over the whirling sound of the drill.

When he finally came to the door, looking preoccupied and barely greeting me, I knew something was wrong. Things were moved around in the studio, and on one of the sculpture stands, hidden under a piece of white sheeting, the shape of a bust was evident. Alexander went back to the crate he'd been opening, started up the hand drill to remove the screws, and then pried open the bin that housed the used Plasticine about to be recycled into William Dzus for the second time.

He didn't have to talk. I understood what had happened. The plaster cast had not been approved, and now he had to try again. The metal armature was back on the stand. Dzus needed to look more optimistic. Staring at the rejected bust, Alexander shook his head. "Not only is he ugly, one eye is lidded." Alexander needed to disguise this problem so that Dzus looked strong and attractive to the workers in his factories where the portraits would be installed.

Within an hour he had deftly built the Plasticine back on the armature and was moving it around in big round blobs. Rejection never set him back. He trusted his own dexterity, and there was always another approach. He might experience fatigue, but never defeat. With the help of his wire end tool and a modeling knife, he re-created the head.

Several times throughout the day, Alexander pulled the cover from the Dzus portrait and puttered with it, trying to cheer up the industrialist's grumpy demeanor. Then, just as quickly, he turned his attention to another task, his movements always deliberate and efficient.

When the mail arrived, he read it immediately and drafted by hand the replies for me to type before returning to the Dzus bust. I spent a few hours typing Alexander's correspondence every day. This gave me insight into his business efforts. In addition to commissions from the Ukrainian patrons, Alexander was actively seeking lecture posts, and secured one in British Columbia for the following August. In the stack of letters that day was more correspondence related to the time-consuming and ultimately fruitless negotiations with the Ukrainian-run Orbit Film Company for a film about Alexander's life and work. Another letter was to his German dealer, Klihm, with whom he was in constant communication, following the progress of his traveling retrospective. Sales occurred, and Alexander continued to complete new pieces to replace those which had sold.

A mountain of Alexander's correspondence has been preserved to this day, helping to trace certain issues as they developed over the years. It was in his letters to Klihm, for example, that Alexander's concerns about forgery began to surface. He noticed that his works were showing up as unauthorized casts, especially as it became public knowledge that the prices of his bronzes were increasing and that the market was growing. In a letter to Klihm, he states: "I obtained photographic proof that somebody [made] false works under my name. Somebody tried to imitate my style. A German museum was the purchaser of this forged work."[1] Unfortunately, this was the beginning of decades of untraceable editions which would plague Archipenko's legacy and materialize into serious questions about the authenticity of much of his work, even during his lifetime.

Initially, he was suspicious of foundries. Over the years, plaster models had been broken, lost, misplaced, or stolen at foundries. Some were used to create unauthorized editions. A foundry, whether a commercial or an art foundry, sees its role in producing art objects very differently than the artist does. As craftspeople, the workers in the foundry feel proprietorship which can be exaggerated. If they followed the market, they would realize that what they were paid was sometimes less than ten percent of the art market price of an object that could not exist in bronze without their craft. Because they had the model on hand, there was good reason to worry about the rules being broken. It wasn't always the foundry owner who was the problem. The underpaid workmen were also vulnerable.

Alexander concluded his letter to Klihm with his own solution: "Such events force me to protect my work as well as the interests of the buyer. As protection I decided to give to each buyer my certificate of authenticity. Please don't deliver work to a buyer without my certificate."[2] Providing a certificate to accompany sales became Alexander's usual practice.

In Alexander's zeal to place his work, the correspondence from the period also suggests that he overstepped some boundaries. One day a letter from Galerie Klihm in Germany arrived, describing attempts to make sales and arrange new locations for the work to be seen in Europe. At the same time, Alexander had a similar, ongoing correspondence with William Semcesen, a Ukrainian art dealer based in Norway who bought bronzes that Alexander would cast especially for him. Throughout the summer of 1956, letters between Archipenko and Semcesen flew back and forth with checklists of available works and prices attached. They communicated about contracts for exhibitions and international representation. They made mutual promises, some of them quite grand, such as a large European touring exhibition that would include the Tate in London and sizable commissions. In the end, little came of their negotiations except confusion, disappointment, and a huge amount of time-consuming and detailed correspondence in Ukrainian. Alexander was drawn to conducting business in the Ukrainian community where, as a famous international figure, he was treated like a star and called "maestro." In my view, this path led to disappointment.

I don't believe that either dealer knew about the other. Just as Klihm was probably doing, Semcesen was contacting people in London and Switzerland. In his thoroughness and drive to leave no opportunity untested, Alexander was unaware of how this relentlessness would be perceived in the coming years.

* * *

As usual, when Alexander was moving from stand to stand in his studio, it was with complete focus. Nothing else mattered. He never heard the slam of a door or the fire trucks that used this part of upper Broadway as a fast route to trouble. He also failed to hear the thud.

Seated in front of the typewriter in the narrow, dimly lit corridor of an office, I leaned forward to get a better look at the handwritten rough draft I was typing. As always, the rooms shook with the rumble of buses, impatient cars honking, and police sirens. In the shadows behind me, it was all but invisible, waiting for its moment. Because my mind was on the letter—I was annoyed at yet another typo that needed white-out—I didn't notice the five-foot high *Vase Woman III (Ray)* (fig. 6) sliding from its unstable place against the wall.

Suddenly, a strange vibration pressed me forward, the rear legs of my chair lifted off the ground, and the back of the chair pressed into my shoulders. I probably wouldn't remember the chair but for its ugly sturdiness, which resisted the weight of the life-size aluminum figure that was now looking smartly over my shoulder, inches from the back of my head. Just that morning the statue had been delivered and temporarily stashed in the hall. Although the object was modeled with extreme delicacy to project a benign, otherworldly presence, it had the shape of a modern weapon and the heft to be fatal.

My heart started to thump. I felt as if lightning had just missed me. I needed to cry but couldn't—because in that split second, I decided I wouldn't. When Alexander walked through the door from the studio a few minutes later, he barely seemed to notice the sculpture pinning my chair against the desk or to register the minute distance between

Fig. 18 Installation view, Darmstadt, Germany, 1955, Archipenko Foundation, Bearsville, NY

Fig. 19 Installation view, Düsseldorf, Germany, 1955, Archipenko Foundation, Bearsville, NY
Fig. 20 Installation view, Recklinghausen, Germany, 1955, Archipenko Foundation, Bearsville, NY

the back of my skull and *Vase Woman III (Ray)*. Although he recognized that I was a bit shaken, once it was clear that I was unharmed, he simply moved the statue to a safer spot and went back to the whir of his jigsaw. The moment was over.

Our unspoken pact to avoid psychodrama remained intact. It seems we both wanted the same thing that day—the emotional strength to allow other things to happen besides a near accident. And our work came first.

That afternoon, the new Dzus portrait was finally completed. The industrialist was now gazing outward, his head tilted up, yet with all the identifying facial lines, wrinkles, and jowls still in place, and Alexander was heading for the door.

"I'll be back soon. I need to get some stamps and make a deposit at the bank." From his correspondence, I knew he'd also just obtained a new portrait commission, a memorial for Luke Myshuha, another famous Ukrainian who had been editor of the newspaper *Svoboda* and a staunch supporter of exiled Ukrainian youth. It was being sponsored by the Ukrainian Institute of America and paid for by Dzus. No wonder Alexander was running to the bank; the $1,000 deposit had arrived in the mail.

When Alexander returned with the stamps and a package from the hardware store—more metal wire for the next armature, which would support the portrait of Myshuha—*Vase Woman III (Ray)* was leaning against a far wall and I was at my workstand, completing the sketches for a bas-relief. This was where I wanted to be. I wouldn't let a brush with death break my routine. Work was my anchor, a cathartic process, and I allowed biomorphic shapes to edit my emotions.

As 1955 came to a close, I fit almost seamlessly into Alexander's life. Our affair was titillating and addictive—a secret we shared. Every time we parted at Grand Central Station, our attraction would grow.

Nevertheless, an uncomfortable sense of confusion was seeping into our lives. Although I couldn't admit it to myself, the deception left me feeling isolated and at odds with the rest of the world. My ongoing relationship with Alexander was the first important thing in my life that I'd kept from my parents and grandparents. I knew all about being discreet, but I'd never before had a reason to be deceptive. Maintaining this secrecy about our relationship was taking a toll on me which I didn't yet understand.

Chapter Five
A Sense of Purpose

Something was very wrong. I'd felt tired when I arrived at the school that morning. Now, at the end of the day, fatigue was closing down on me, becoming heavier and heavier. Unable to concentrate or complete a project, I began hearing sounds in between sounds, and colors started to bounce. The moment it began, I was fearful that this was an echo of what had happened when I was fourteen. I found it difficult to talk, my breathing felt shallow, and I was tearful without feeling sad. Everything was vibrating and generating an aura. Suddenly the studio was very crowded and I couldn't move. The colors and sounds were in the way.

Although I managed to find my way to the desk chair and told myself the breakdown wouldn't be noticed by anyone else, I couldn't find the words to put a sentence together to explain what was happening. I was dissociating, but I didn't know why. I sat immobilized, knowing I was unable to make it to Grand Central and the commuter train. Alexander's reaction was similar to the one he had if I put a full glass on the edge of a table without thinking. He'd know I was off and catch the glass. He called my father to collect me by car for the drive back to Scarsdale.

Both Alexander and I had been under pressure as 1956 progressed. Angelica's worsening medical condition required her to be hospitalized, and the only option they had was a charity hospital on Welfare Island. While Alexander had been pleased with the exposure and sales from his six-city show in Germany, it was now ending. Except for the exhibition at the university in Pennsylvania, no new shows were scheduled until the Perls exhibition, a year away. Klaus Perls, the president of the Art Dealers Association of America, was to become Alexander's major US dealer. Perhaps prompted by the European stir caused by the touring exhibition in Germany (figs. 18,19, 20), Perls was planning a 1957 solo show of Archipenko's newer polychrome works at his gallery on Madison Avenue. This show had the potential to rehabilitate Alexander's US reputation and bring sales. For now, though, the work that he was interested in doing would have to wait. More frantic than ever about his finances, he relentlessly pursued commissions, mainly portraiture, and actively sought dealers in Europe. Although his efforts eventually led to shows in Switzerland, England, and Italy, those exhibitions were all in the future.

My breakdown was initially physical—sheer fatigue—but on a deeper level, the dissociation may have been psychological, the result of juggling contradictory emotions. I was feeling burdened not only by the weight of conducting a secret affair, but also by the pressure of Alexander's faith in me as an artist. As he confronted mortality in the illness of his wife, he seemed to unconsciously look to me to repeat his own trajectory at a young age. I did not always welcome this pressure. Alexander wanted to show my work to curators and art dealers, telling me, "Frances, there's no reason you shouldn't have early fame as I did. I'll help you, because your work deserves it."

His belief in my talent had led me into a kind of work rapture. When he said, "If you're an artist, you need to exhibit your work. You're accumulating enough work to look for a dealer," I worked even harder. Soon I was spending twelve hours a day in the studio, eating sporadically and never at rest, feverishly absorbed in making art. At the end of the day my arms and legs ached. By the time I dropped into a chair, I would crumple like a rag doll.

Although I believed in what I was doing, the professional side of art felt remote and premature. I wasn't convinced about launching a career or finding an audience. Elevation to "fame" seemed artificial, not natural. It was Alexander's need more than mine. Alexander wanted to lead and to excel—that was his nature. As his own career was nearing its end, he may have unconsciously hoped that I would become an extension. I couldn't tell him that I didn't feel ready, because I didn't want to stop the process. I didn't want to disconnect.

My stress may also have come from the growing pains I was experiencing as I struggled to trade my family's belief system for the one I craved. The two different messages that I was hearing—one from my family and the other from Alexander—were at odds. My family background encouraged me to believe that my security was not dependent upon professional success but social success, which meant getting married to someone who would be a good provider. In contrast, I wanted my work to be integrated with my values—and I didn't value my parents' version of life. What they thought was important seemed very superficial. For me, going to the country club was a kind of not being.

I felt that my artwork must express something on a higher level or my life wasn't worth living. Above all, Alexander's work articulated a higher purpose. Archipenko's commitment to his art had a moral purpose, reflecting universal truths and laws. For him, the artist was merely a conduit for this elevated consciousness. I wasn't just modeling myself as a stylish, educated New Yorker. When I was making art, I experienced a sense of purpose. I was replacing conventional values with deeper ones that weren't political or social, but metaphysical. What I was doing, I believed, was very, very important: art was self-perpetuating, even if Alexander's pushiness felt like fingernails on a chalkboard. If anything, I now believed that I, too, could be a conduit.

That I might dismiss people who weren't producing "meaningful work" signaled a slow erosion of my humanity. At a core level, I agreed with Alexander's belief that personal relationships were secondary to art. This principle underlay all his relationships, past and present, including his deeply personal ones. Continually absorbed in the experience of being an artist and the lover of an amazing one, my sense of self became inflated. Although I easily find commonality and empathy today, at that time I was unable to connect with people. It was enough for me to know that a real human being whom I could respect was completely invested in me and my work. Alexander's belief in me was an intoxicant.

This attention from my mentor and lover also led me to believe that I had a central role in his life. Certainly he was central to mine. I knew I was at least one of the positive things in his life and that it was rare to be that for someone else. As I look back now, though, I think I may have been only a distraction from his financial struggles and his ill wife. I was never a direct inspiration for his work and was clearly not his muse. I never posed for him, nor did he ever name anything after me in the way that Angelica inspired him to name works after her. Almost sixty years later, I sometimes imagine that perhaps I served as an amusement that could give him some temporary pleasure, like a concert or a museum exhibition. At the time, however, I couldn't afford to face the idea that he could be in the category of men I was rejecting, those with conventional notions of male superiority, offering women roles as "pets" or mascots.

Whether I subconsciously recognized this or whether some internal conflict came to the surface under the pressure of physical fatigue, my sense of self suddenly shifted. "Depleted from fatigue" was my mother's diagnosis. Fortunately, she didn't overthink what was happening. My parents still had no idea that Alexander and I were anything more than teacher and student. However, they were beginning to sense that I didn't want to be an upper-middle-class bourgeois married to a doctor with wall-to-wall carpeting in Westchester. For me to disappear from the upper middle class would mean something was very wrong with me and reflect back as if something were very wrong with them, too. In reality, if I was involved with my teacher, they didn't want to know. Aside from the fact that Alexander was fifty years older than me and an artist rather than a doctor, my having a sexual "relationship" outside of marriage would also be cause for embarrassment. I had failed to land my man. A woman's goal in their milieu was to catch a man like you caught a fish.

A change of scene and complete rest were my mother's remedy for my lost stability. Soon I was aboard ship on a cruise to Bermuda.

When I returned from my rest cure after ten days—physically renewed, the episode over—Alexander and I never spoke of my breakdown or even my absence. As if nothing had occurred, we headed for Woodstock where Angelica, who'd been released from the hospital for the summer, always welcomed me to tea.

After my evenings with Alexander in the studio, I slept in my blue bedroom in the house and he stayed in the cottage with his wife. Even when Alexander and I became lovers and eventually married, I recognized that she had been the love of his life. I accepted that Alexander and I were connected in a different way. When he was quite young, he had painted an icon with a face that looked like mine. Perhaps there was a physicality about me that reminded him of something early in his life, maybe someone who looked like me long before I was born.

Our deep connection was our art, and our lives proceeded in the same mutually understood way. After my "episode," we were rarely apart again. I was his hope of reliving his lost and famous youth, and he was my inspiration. But at the end of our first year together, this arrangement was not without conflict.

* * *

"That's beautiful. How'd you do it?" Coming from his studio, where he'd been working out formulas amidst bottles of powdered pigments and various chemicals, Alexander joined me in the little side garden. The blowtorch was set up and my sculpture was cooling. When we'd arrived in Woodstock that summer, in 1956, Alexander had sent two of my pieces with his to be cast in bronze, and I'd been putting all my effort into making one of my statuettes perfect.

To keep the noise of the rotating tool and the dust away from the workspace of the other students, we had rolled a small workbench with a vise and extension cord into the yard, and Alexander lent me tools to get me started. I felt as set apart and special as my statue.

I'd spent the week saturated with metal dust, and my hands were tired from using the noisy, vibrating, rotating disc, followed by hand tools to smooth or "chase" the seams in the statue. The trick was to neither take off nor leave too much, and I had the plaster model beside me to refer to. Not only was I learning a specific technique, but more importantly, I was learning the discipline of consistent effort. Although some modern sculptors, such as Brancusi, preferred to do their own chasing, it's essentially busywork. When Alexander could afford to, he had the foundry do the finishing.

That morning, as I'd started splashing the diluted acids on the hot surface of the bronze, I understood one of Alexander's early pronouncements: "Art is ninety percent day labor." Achieving color was dependent on the sequence and amount of liquid and heat. I stippled the different acids on with a brush one after another and then removed them with a wet sponge before heating the bronze again with a loud whoosh from the blowtorch. Since my sculpture was small, this was quite easy and quick to do with a couple of brushes, sponges, and a bucket of water. Soon, I had built up several thin layers of overlapping colors that were nuanced. I was like a child playing with finger paints—except this was fire and acid. As water evaporated from the bronze surface, the copper nitrate and iron nitrate smelled like a New York subway on a hot day.

Although every layer of my clothing was saturated with the tint of bronze oxidation and the chemicals permeated my skin and hair, I was exhilarated as the metal began turning a sea green. Students usually aren't encouraged to cast their early efforts in bronze unless they are wealthy, so I'd been anxious. I didn't want to disappoint my teacher.

Now Alexander and I were both staring at the result. Clearly surprised at the professional-looking surface of my statue, he looked around for a notebook. "Let's see your notes."

I shrugged. What I'd achieved was clearly beginner's luck. "I don't have any." I'd taken an intuitive risk rather than being studiously respectful of the elements. But I didn't know what I was doing or remember exactly what method or mixture I'd used to achieve the verdigris patina.

"You didn't keep notes? What's the formula?" Alexander scowled.

I stepped closer to my statue. "I was just playing. It was an accident."

Lowering his voice, he looked at me in an odd way. "You must give me your notes." He was serious. He didn't believe it had happened by chance. For months he'd been struggling with the patina on pieces that were larger than mine. Perhaps maintaining the correct surface heat was part of his problem. But I wouldn't say that. I still believed that I didn't know anything and he knew everything.

Now it was all topsy-turvy and very upsetting. He assumed I had notes and wasn't sharing them? Was it jealousy? Ironically, of course, my work imitated his approach. He was also accusing me of not being serious. His anger made me feel defensive, undermined, raw, disconnected, even assaulted. We began to raise our voices, and soon we were both yelling. I grabbed my bronze, which had now cooled, threw it into a pile of weeds, and ran off in tears. In doing this, I probably startled myself even more than Alexander.

I don't think Alexander even saw the incident as a fight. When I finished crying in my bedroom and returned to the studio, he joked with me and made my favorite dinner. Alexander knew his women well. We settled down over a large plate of spaghetti with a tomato sauce that he concocted combining lots of garlic with fresh wild mint he picked outside the studio.

On some level, of course, the student was outgrowing the teacher. I see in hindsight that his pride in my accomplishments was tempered with a touch of possessiveness as he watched me advance. Ultimately, however, Alexander continued his enthusiasm for my career. The next day he nodded at a finished wood carving in the corner on a stand. "Put that aside." Then he turned to one of my small polychrome statues. "You should add that one." Art teachers promoting their students was routine in the 1950s, and probably still is. It was not unusual for Archipenko to suggest that I submit my pieces to shows which he'd been asked to jury. With the afternoon light warming the Woodstock studio, he silently critiqued as he moved along. It was too late to make suggestions. These were finished works. Finally, remaining very still, he spoke without looking at me. "Frances, you have enough for a show."

A sense of dread which I didn't quite understand passed over me. Finally I simply said, "Thank you." Being totally speechless was more embarrassing than crying. Now Alexander was urging me to prepare for an exhibition and show dealers my work. I was numb. I didn't know how these things worked, but I had to believe him. I was an outsider, and he was my one source. I trusted him.

The immediate problem I faced was space. The summer was over. In a week we'd be leaving for New York, where there would be restrictions on what I could do. I wouldn't have the freedom of Woodstock. Rotating between several projects, I was taking up too much room in the New York school, and I needed a workspace where I could use power tools without disturbing the other students.

At the other end of the Lincoln Arcade, a small corner studio with a sink and windows facing Broadway had become available. Although the studio was tiny, the height and the view gave the illusion of space. Two of the walls were actually high windows which met at the corner of 65th and Broadway. From there, I would be able to see Columbus Circle and bake in the noon sun. I just had to find a way to pay for it.

* * *

My grandfather arrived alone at the Archipenko Art School and knocked on the open door before entering. Well-groomed, he had the demeanor of an art patron with his hat and cane. In contrast, Alexander greeted him wearing a work apron, with worker's hands. They were almost the same age, both first-generation immigrants. And not only were they from the same city, Kiev, but they had both fled at about the same time. Standing on the sidelines, I watched as their paths crossed in New York City under such odd circumstances.

When I'd asked my grandfather if I could exchange the fur coat for cash to rent my own studio, he hadn't been angry. He was proud. Without stating it directly, he'd always encouraged my independence from my parents' priorities. Sometimes, my grandfather would take me aside and say, "You are the smartest person in the family." I think he meant the wisest. This was his ongoing secret conversation with me.

I was the only one in the family who would reject his gifts of money. I'd thank him and ask him to keep it for me until I needed it. Now I needed it. And he was happy to become my patron. However, there was a caveat. I was a bit taken aback when he said, "I'll give you money to get a studio. But can I see what you're doing, meet your teacher, and see the space?"

I needn't have worried. The rapport between Alexander and my grandfather was instant. Perhaps it was generational, or because they were from the same Russian city. Maybe they sensed they were both outsiders, not educated as Americans, looking into a society that would never be their own. Popular culture in the form of film, radio, and advertising was a daily reminder of this to both of them. Alexander had bridged the society gap by achieving international fame. That Alexander was the real thing, my grandfather recognized immediately. He didn't need it confirmed by art historians.

Before departing, my grandfather looked around the Lincoln Arcade and made one comment about where I was spending all my time: "It's just as well you don't wear a good fur coat in this place. You might get robbed. Promise me you will be careful and not take chances."

My grandfather, whose success had been in real estate, made sure that the landlord gave me the best deal. The rent was taken care of for a year and, instead of wearing the coat purchased to secure me an Ivy League husband, I was committed to wearing my old cloth coat for another season. That was fine. I loved my new studio.

* * *

It was an Indian summer afternoon in late September 1956. The windows were open to the car horns on Broadway as Alexander started with a small sketch, enlarged his ideas on brown wrapping paper, and cut the pieces out as templates. Next he taped the brown-paper shapes onto sheets of gleaming commercial Formica and chromium-plated metal, both of which he'd collected on our scavenging trips to Canal Street. Soon the floor of the studio was vibrating from his circular saw grinding against the Formica.

Watching Alexander make decisions always interested me. He allowed himself to make mistakes by taking chances. With this new piece, he certainly knew he was taking a chance. *Revolving Figure (The Art of Reflection)* (fig. 21) was a multi-material rotating construction over six feet high that was to be installed at the 1956 Annual Exhibition at

Fig. 21 Alexander Archipenko, *Revolving Figure (The Art of Reflection)*, 1956, wood, mother of pearl, and metal, 78 in. (198.1 cm), Frances Gray Collection

the Whitney Museum in November. As with much of his experimental work, the form and materials contained innate symbolism. In the simplicity of the construction—four intersecting planes merged together at right angles and were mounted on an elevated, rotating base—Alexander evoked his interest in movement, orbiting patterns, and reflection. The choice of media merged past and future cultures. On the plywood surfaces, each one differently shaped, he veneered Formica and chromed metal, and on the other planes he glued pieces of abalone shell, thus integrating natural and industrial materials as he had in *Oceanic Madonna*.

* * *

When we arrived, the entrance to the Whitney Museum was puffed up with guards taking tickets and people blowing kisses. I was surprised to see that there were even photographers clicking cameras at us.

As we moved through the galleries and met up with some of Alexander's former students, several collectors of his work, and a handful of acquaintances, I listened and smiled but rarely talked. Alexander clearly enjoyed how I looked and the way I looked at people and things. I was also conscious that he politely introduced me as "a gifted young sculptress." He didn't say "student."

We were all herded into the freight-sized elevator to be let off at the exhibition floor, where *Revolving Figure (The Art of Reflection)* was the first work we saw. Alexander's installation was an object all dressed up that had finally found a place to go— even if it was just for a short visit. The other pieces at the Whitney Annual looked morbid and a bit stale in comparison. It was a bad year for sculpture. Alexander noticed a work by Sue Fuller made of thread and generously concluded: "A spider would be jealous." Lu Duble, one of Alexander's former students who attended the show, took the cake for negative titles that year with *Dark Reaper*.

Among a potpourri of works from Alexander Calder to Joseph Cornell, Archipenko's piece drew the most attention.

Something unexpected among the mostly grim academic work then going on in New York, it was the only sculpture reviewed in *The New York Times* by Howard Devree. His faint praise was accurate, if nothing else. Devree commented, "The sculpture section (forty three examples) in the Whitney is smaller than usual and, this reviewer feels, less rewarding than in recent years. . . . For sheer novelty a sculpture by Alexander Archipenko will probably attract much attention."[1] It was easy to find if you were looking for it. Not only was it large, it was in motion.

In Vancouver three months earlier, Archipenko had been welcomed by the local press as the most important sculptor of the twentieth century—as important to sculpture as Picasso was to painting. He had been invited to lecture at the University of British Columbia at the same time Sir Herbert Read was participating in its summer program, indicating Alexander's continued status among European intellectuals of a certain vintage.

Especially in New York, however, which was so different from the intellectual bohemia of Paris or the avant-garde of Berlin, Alexander had become increasingly isolated. His path did not include a shift toward Abstract Expressionism. Rather than being recognized as innovative and the harbinger of positive new developments, his experiments with modern materials—such as *Revolving Figure*—led to his growing alienation from the art world that had typecast him as "Cubist" and now rejected his work as "sheer novelty."

For Alexander, the newness of *Revolving Figure* was part of the point. The fresh combination of man-made and natural materials providing reflection and opalescence in this large kinetic object implied a recombining of the spiritual with the mundane. *Revolving Figure* would later be shown at Archipenko's 1957 exhibition at the Perls Galleries.

The Whitney opening was my first meeting with Klaus Perls, the dealer who figured heavily in Alexander's late career and final legacy, eventually functioning as a nemesis to both. At the time, however, Alexander was pleased to be shown by one of the leading art dealers in New York City, who was also well connected in Europe. Once Perls endorsed Archipenko, other dealers and collectors started to show an interest, including Gerald Cramer from Geneva and Wilhelm Grosshennig from Düsseldorf. Perls also introduced Alexander to his colleague Eric Estorick, a Brooklyn-born London dealer who proposed becoming Alexander's European dealer.

Within weeks, a cat-and-mouse game between Estorick and Archipenko had begun, a game that would continue throughout their seven-year relationship and end in recriminations and rupture. The conflict with Estorick began with one particular early plaster model, *Geometric Statuette*, 1914 (fig. 22). In a letter dated December 5, 1956, Estorick suggested that he and Alexander "make an arrangement between us" for casting the statue in bronze.[2]

As would eventually surface, even though Estorick had the plaster in his hands, he didn't own it. It was part of the Goeritz collection, a large group of early Archipenko works which Erich Goeritz (who had since died) had housed for safekeeping in the Tel Aviv Museum during World War II. Acting as a front man for the Goeritz family in London, Estorick convinced the son, Andrew, to allow an edition of bronzes to be made from this early plaster. Insinuating that *Geometric Statuette* belonged to him, Estorick then sought Alexander's permission to make three copies.

On February 6, 1957, Alexander replied, "Concerning the casting of my statue, I think it should be done for the sake of preservation. If you are planning to come to New York, perhaps you can bring the plaster statue along to be cast here. . . . I will be glad to supervise the work."[3] Over a year later, a formal contract was signed, Estorick officially became Alexander's dealer, and *Geometric Statuette* was cast in bronze by Estorick, not Archipenko—creating a major controversy in their volatile relationship. Although Alexander was wary, he couldn't possibly know that Estorick would figure in the coming scandals over unauthorized sculptures that would plague his last years and his reputation.

Even though history would confirm that Alexander was right to question Perls and his network, for now, Alexander was happy to have European dealers seeking to represent his work and a solo show about to take place on Madison Avenue.

Fig. 22 Alexander Archipenko,
Geometric Statuette, 1914, plaster,
20⅝ in. (52.4 cm), Triton Foundation

Chapter Six
Our Third Summer

Most mornings when I stopped by Alexander's studio during the winter and spring of 1957, the power saw was on, the sun was highlighting the dust in the air, brushes were soaking, and the entire room smelled of paint thinner. Carefully positioned about the studio were materials pulled from the bins on Canal Street: Formica, aluminum, metal. Poised on a shelf waiting their turn were solvents, powdered pigments, glues, courtesy samples of SculptMetal, and house paints purchased from the local hardware store. Alexander loved to tinker with new materials. Unfazed by the ambivalent response to the multi-material *Revolving Figure* at the Whitney, he never doubted his own judgment. Although his importance was associated with his well-known early sculptures, Alexander's irreverent multimedia pieces came from his own particular theorizing and odd sensibility—very different from the current trends. He wasn't playing to an audience. He was doing.

From early morning until late afternoon, Alexander alternated his attention between several large multi-material constructions in various stages of assembly. He had positioned his wall reliefs—which he labeled "sculpto-paintings"—throughout the studio according to whether they were just cut, ready for a specific treatment, or waiting for the next stage. Outside the open window, the spring air brought in the familiar sounds of the street, and an industrial fan added to the din.

These sculpto-paintings usually began with sketches, frequently notated with instructions as to colors or materials and sometimes graphed out for enlargement (fig. 23). The final work was often quite similar to the initial concept. The drawings were precious to Alexander, as were his sketches starting from the 1930s for sculptures, marked with red x's on the page, to be realized later (fig. 24). These sketches were different in intent from a series of other drawings done to memorialize finished sculptures. Sometimes rather than an initial sketch, the material he found on Canal Street might be the inspiration for a new idea. The relief *White* may have simply been suggested by white Bakelite, a material upon which he was able to engrave and draw (figs. 25, 26). The sketches for *Multi-Colored Figure* contained notes for his initial plan, but materials he had lying around

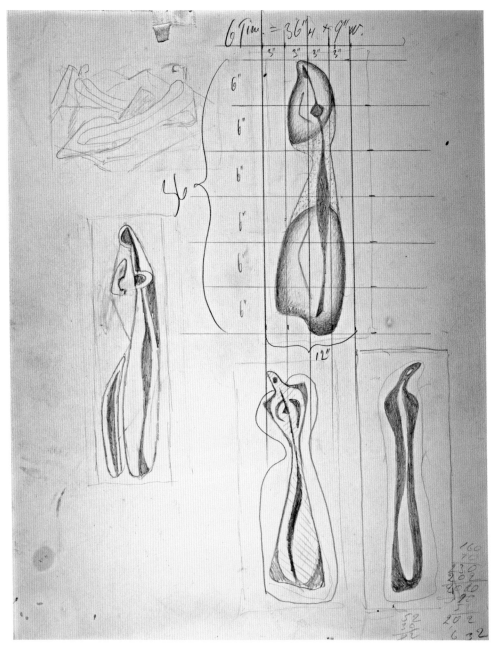

Fig. 23 Alexander Archipenko, *Sketch for Orange and Black*, 1957, pencil on thick paper, 10⁷/₈ x 13¹⁵/₁₆ in. (27.6 x 35.4 cm), Frances Gray Collection

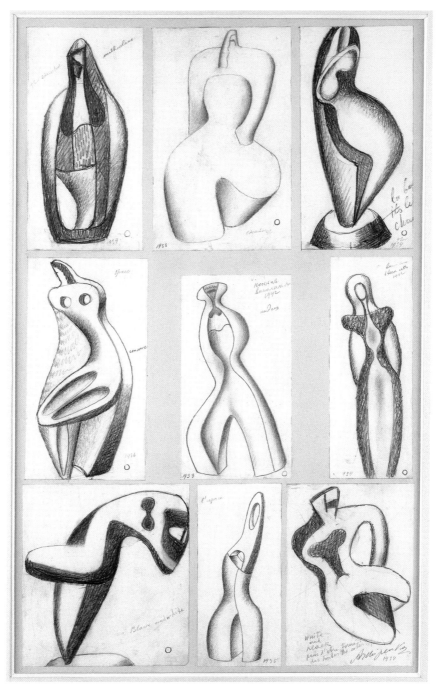

Fig. 24 Alexander Archipenko, *Nine Work Sketches for Sculpture II*, 1934, pencil and ink, framed, 29¼ x 18⅝ in. (93 x 65.5 cm), Frances Gray Collection

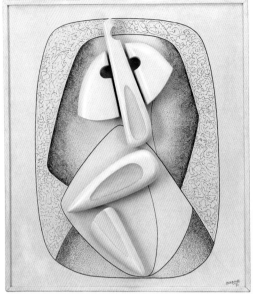
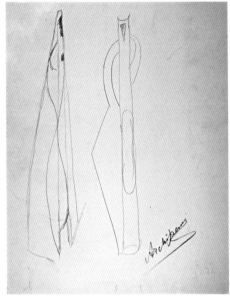

Fig. 25 Alexander Archipenko, *White*, 1957, wood, Bakelite, and paint, 43 x 37 x 3½ in. (109.2 x 94 x 9 cm), Frances Gray Collection
Fig. 26 Alexander Archipenko, *Sketch for White*, 1957, pencil, 10⅞ x 13¹⁵/₁₆ in. (27.6 x 35.4 cm), Frances Gray Collection

the studio altered and determined the final piece (figs. 27, 28). Alexander also used the same materials in different ways—or at least in different works. The Bakelite in *Red* (fig. 29) was the same material that he used in *Cleopatra* (fig. 30) and *Orange and Black* (fig. 31). However, in *Red* he used a dentist's drill and small rotating polishing stones to remove the red surface skin and reveal the base material, which he then textured and gently contoured.

As I worked on one of the higher floors of the southern wing of the Lincoln Arcade Building, my art became the glue that kept me whole. I moved between stands and tables in my own studio, working on several projects at once. By this time I knew how to use power tools and install metal shelves; I had a carving bench with a good vise and a sculpture stand on wheels; and I was adept at building armatures and casting plaster. After spending hours on one figure, I'd cover it and put it aside. Alexander had taught me good studio practices by example.

Using the box of blue glass we'd found on Canal Street, I created a mosaic in my bas-relief *Aeolus* (fig. 32). The background for this piece is beaten lead, suggesting a leaden sky. On the blue glass mosaic, a raised abstract figure becomes a soaring, carved and painted airborne creature. I didn't have to know where the idea for the construction came from. Rather than being stimulated by a specific image, Alexander had taught me to stay open to the swirl of images in my subconscious and to accept what floated to the surface. I had free-associated when I picked up a pen and trusted my intuition, an approach Alexander encouraged. In building an idea, new materials that one has never used before might suggest themselves, as in the case of the blue glass and *Aeolus*. Even in selecting the title, I followed Alexander's example, finding a narrative description to enrich the experience of the actual piece. I was soaring. Work was pleasure. And so was watching Alexander. Although we now had separate studios, we were still aware of each other's progress as we met up at the school in the evenings.

As the New York summer sun began to heat up the windows, the grinding noises of the studio no longer blocked out the sound of the 66th Street crosstown bus. While a dozen finished multi-material works were being covered for their eventual blanket-wrapped move across town for the exhibition at the Perls Galleries, we left for Woodstock, where Alexander completed the list for the show.

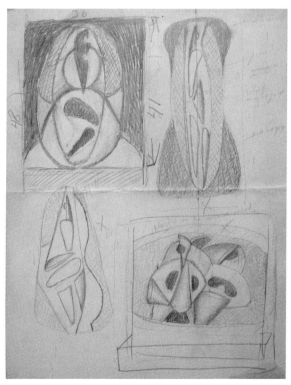 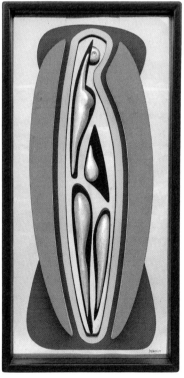

Fig. 27 Alexander Archipenko, *Sketch for Multi-Colored Figure*, 1957, pencil, 10⁷/₈ x 13¹⁵/₁₆ in. (27.6 x 35.4 cm), Frances Gray Collection
Fig. 28 Alexander Archipenko, *Multi-Colored Figure*, 1957, wood, metal, and Bakelite, 51³/₄ x 23³/₄ in. (131.5 x 65.5 x 18 cm), Frances Gray Collection

Although he would eventually stop using acrylic glass as a medium, particles of toxic dust became permanently embedded in the cracks of the wooden floor as Alexander finished *Spirit*, the acrylic-glass sculpture he'd been working on the summer I met him (fig. 4).

Alexander wasn't the first artist to use contemporary materials, but in his practice he was never of the same mind as the Russian Futurists or Constructivists, who had a political agenda. Not interested in reducing his art practice to specific visual elements or mere political and psychological expressions, he sought to achieve the broadest and deepest expression of ultimate truths. László Moholy-Nagy, Archipenko's colleague at the Chicago New Bauhaus, also worked with acrylic glass as a designer, using it as part of constructions that could then be photographed to portray the variations of light and its movement. In the 1920s, Moholy-Nagy also started to use synthetic materials such as aluminum, celluloid, and opaque plastics in experiments with photo collages, which he called "photo-plastics." The early Dadaists, in their rejection of materialism, also worked with multi-materials, found objects, collage, and simplified geometric forms, but scoffed at the spiritual in art.

For Alexander, the transmission of light that carved acrylic glass permitted also created an implied expression of the spiritual. The title *Spirit* leaves us with no doubt of his intent. Henri Bergson's philosophy and Albert Einstein's theory of relativity inspired Archipenko's generation of European artists and followed them wherever they immigrated. In Archipenko's book *Fifty Creative Years*, as well as in his teaching, his approach was to elevate his art practice to the spiritual and align it with the universal. He never rejected or undermined the object. The visual arts, he believed, produced objects that were in a sense talismans of civilization, and he would establish a new art legacy by adding contemporary materials to traditional ones. Alexander aimed at the sublime, whether his medium was Bakelite or marble. Several small works in bronze and two terra-cotta figures completed the work going to the Perls show.

While Alexander was creating noise and dust in his studio, I began the summer outside under the beechnut tree carving in wood. *Red Jester* (fig. 33), like most of my work in wood, was from mahogany, the wood easiest to carve. However, I spent the majority of the summer learning a new skill from Alexander: carving marble. The piece of white marble which Alexander gave me was one of two discarded tombstones. The first Alexander had used in 1952 to carve his *Lazarus* (fig. 34). This second piece—which was sometimes used as a doorstop—became my experiment and lesson in stone carving. As I worked outside, keeping the dust away from the other students' workspace, the simple, almost prehistoric image of a mother and child conforming to the size and shape of the marble took the remainder of the summer for me to complete. It would be the one and

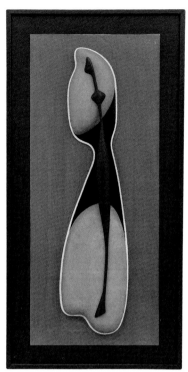

Fig. 29 Alexander Archipenko, *Red*, 1957, wood, Bakelite, turquoise, and paint, 49½ x 39½ x 6½ in. (125.7 x 100.3 x 16.5 cm),
Frances Gray Collection

Fig. 30 Alexander Archipenko, *Cleopatra*, 1957, wood, Bakelite, and found objects, 38 x 84 in. (96.5 x 213.4 cm), Frances Gray Collection

Fig. 31 Alexander Archipenko, *Orange and Black*, 1957, wood, metal, and Bakelite, 48¾ x 25 x 4 in. (123.8 x 63.5 x 10.2 cm),
Frances Gray Collection

Fig. 32 Frances Gray, *Aeolus*, 1956, wood, mosaic, and lead, 31 x 24 x 5 in. (78.7 x 61 x 12 cm), Frances Gray Collection
Fig. 33 Frances Gray, *Red Jester*, 1957, wood and lead, 60 in. (152.4 cm), Frances Gray Collection

only marble statue I ever wanted to make. Titled *Mother and Child* (fig. 35, right), it was included in my first solo show.

In the summer evenings—once Angelica had dinner and was settled—I joined Alexander in his studio and continued to type his manuscript while he improvised on the piano. At the end of the night, he would gently steer me away from the typewriter toward the little room where the queen-size bed waited, and he'd write stories on my back or recall tales of his early years.

His descriptions of prewar Paris were just decadent enough from a distance to be intriguing. Upon arrival, he quickly ran out of money, subsisting on salted herring to keep his belly full and camping out in a barrel near the Seine to keep warm and dry. Once he had a studio, he would work nonstop for two weeks at a time, having meals brought in and cutting himself off from everything social so that he could work without interruption. Afterwards, he'd devote the following two weeks to drinking, studio visits, and parties—with intensity. Before he left Moscow, a Russian girlfriend who was a pharmacist had given him some drugs in case he ran out of money and was hungry. He never sold the drugs or used them himself. Instead, he held on to them and later gave them to Modigliani. With controlled abandon was how I perceived he'd lived his life. His descriptions were so vivid that I sometimes felt I was part of his ongoing narrative; at other times I was the audience. Either way, I looked forward to our time together after the studio noises ceased, Angelica was cared for, and the students were relaxing in their quarters.

* * *

Eventually, the buzz of the insects changed to a deeper sound, trill-like, as if all the small creatures were anticipating a change of electricity in the air. Even the drying of the leaves made the air feel different and announced that summer, our third one together, was ending once again.

We were alone in Alexander's studio in the fall of 1957, the windows open, the space empty. The summer's work had just been blanketed and picked up by the art movers. Slowly, Alexander started kicking his moving dolly across the floor and watching it pick up speed, hit the opposite floor trim, and rebound at an angle. As he transformed the floor of the studio into a playground which imitated the action on a pool table—but not quite—I tried to stay out of his way. He was up to something which gave me the same discomfort as when he was dangling from a ladder off the roof.

Soon he was sliding across the studio floor on top of the dolly, very nonchalantly for a senior citizen. Alexander had a wit which on occasion was Chaplinesque, and the open space was an invitation for him to mount the empty dolly and see where it might take him. Luckily, he had remarkable physical coordination. His sense of gravity was low, his

Fig. 34 Alexander Archipenko, *Lazarus*, 1952, marble, 23¼ x 13½ x 3⅝ in. (59.1 x 34.3 x 9.2 cm), Frances Gray Collection

Fig. 35 Frances Gray, *Mother and Child* (pictured in right foreground next to Alexander Archipenko's *Mâ Meditation*), 1957 [size not recorded], Archipenko Foundation, Bearsville, NY

hips loose; he was balanced. Managing a controlled speed, he was able to angle before he met the wall. "You should try this—it's really easy."

Finally he got off and gave me a chance. While I admired his ability to negotiate a balancing act, it was not so easy to imitate him. I was afraid. My center of gravity was very different, as was my confidence. When we returned to New York, I would be commuting from Scarsdale once again, trying to juggle and balance my private and public lives.

Although Alexander could always make me laugh, at the same time, I was experiencing the background static of anxiety. This had little to do with the unconventional and secret nature of our relationship. I was always at Alexander's side, but our connection remained undefined and ambiguous, not just to the rest of the world, but to us. Much was left unsaid in our conversations. I told myself that Alexander and I were working artists first and that our personal relationship was "temporary." However, I now realize it was not the secrecy of our relationship that created the growing stress I felt; it was adjusting to the energy I needed to maintain myself in a state of not knowing— and still breathing with ease at all times.

Even if neither of us knew what the other felt, I also found being insecure refreshing and not unwelcome. Never knowing what to expect—as on that last day in Woodstock—

I was jolted by his verve and never in a state of boredom. Alexander knew how to be light. If he took risks, he did not perceive them as such.

As we left for New York, Alexander felt very confident about his new work. For him, the marriage of the material with the spiritual/immaterial never ended. It was integrated with who he was. In one way, the art market shift away from Modernism to Abstract Expressionism had spurred an extremely productive and innovative but little known period for Archipenko, the artist who had been described as the most important innovative sculptor of the century.

Although medical bills continued to drain all his resources, for the 1957 Perls show Alexander hadn't played to the market or compromised his inner vision for the social and economic dependency that framed art and many artists.

* * *

As people drifted in from the street, the Perls Galleries started to hum. The crowd was a mixture, sprinkled with elegant Upper East Side patrons, artistic types less formally dressed, and some students. Alexander's sculptures looked wonderful, like children who have been cleaned and groomed. They gleamed under the gallery lights, set up on freshly painted pedestals or enclosed in glass cabinets. Everything was polished; even the well-waxed floors gleamed from buffing.

Klaus Perls greeted us, his tall, erect presence framed by the formal wrought iron door and his ruddy nose and German accent permeated with breath mints. As always, Archipenko and Perls maintained a formality, rarely addressing each other by their first names. This represented an older generation's approach, in which long-standing professional colleagues used titles. It defined boundaries. When Perls occasionally did call Archipenko "Alexander," I was annoyed by what I saw as a trespass. In effect, Perls seemed to be saying, "I am not only your patron, but your superior." These thoughts may have been indicative of my own confused and oversensitive frame of mind—or perhaps they were some kind of incarnation of a canary in a coal mine.

Alexander, however, was unperturbed as he mingled with the crowd, many of whom had received the gallery's flyer about the show and were moving from one opening to another along Madison Avenue. Genuinely happy to see former students and other artists, Alexander greeted everyone he knew by name, chatting and smiling. Although Angelica was too fragile to attend, even in a wheelchair, I imagined she would enjoy his report of events when he returned home to her later that night. Watching Alexander devote most of his resources, financial and emotional, to Angelica—who'd become totally dependent on him—encouraged me to trust him even more as a compassionate human being.

Alexander and I kept our public appearances low-key—and that included tonight. As I watched collectors and friends view all twenty-six works on display, I moved with them as one of the crowd. In addition to the eight wall reliefs dated 1957, identified in the catalogue separately as "sculpto-paintings," there were multi-material constructions and works in acrylic glass, terra-cotta, aluminum, wood, bronze, and marble. Their size ranged from six and a half to ninety-six inches high. I couldn't help feeling protective of these pieces. They'd all been completed in just three years of production, between 1954 and 1957, and in most cases, I'd been present at their conception.

For *Orange and Black* (fig. 31), I'd watched as Alexander used SculptMetal, a putty-like substance that was easily available, perhaps for the first time. He polished it to a smooth surface before painting it black. Also in this piece, Alexander used the back side of a Bakelite remnant that doesn't appear again in any other work. The final touch for *Black, White and Red* (fig. 36), which the viewer may miss, is that the parallel lines which animate the work were made from soldering metal. Alexander painted this work with premixed house paint and used easily bent aluminum strips to attach everything together. I saw *Multi-Colored Figure* (fig. 28) differently each time I looked at it, depending on my angle of approach, the lighting, and its context.

Although there were no red dots indicating sales, I knew that work didn't necessarily sell at an opening. If Perls had presold a piece to one of his collectors, it would more likely happen at a private viewing, not at the opening. Alexander's patrons were more likely to purchase a work later, from the artist's studio. Perls understood this and might send a good client directly to the studio. In essence, the works in the show were on consignment. It was a trial run for both of them. Perls's diminutive wife, Dolly, sat smoking a cigarillo at a desk in the last gallery. I assumed she was there to quote prices on request.

It appeared that Perls's plan for the show was to build a base for Alexander. His collectors were conservative. They bought blue-chip items, and Perls was presenting Archipenko in that context. This is probably why Perls changed the name of *Cleopatra* (fig. 30) to *Repose*—the title of a work Archipenko had exhibited in the famous 1913 Armory Show. Perls wanted an object with a title which could be identified with a signature piece. Titles referring to narratives were probably not an easy selling point. For

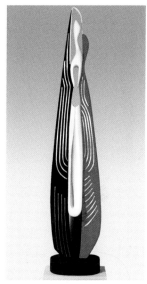

Fig. 36 Alexander Archipenko, *Black, White and Red,* 1957, wood, metal, and paint, 68 in. (172.7 cm), private collection courtesy of Galerie Gmurzynska

instance, the title *Cleopatra* might signal the cinema and popular culture to his clients—not an image that would help impress the critics, who already had preconceived notions about Alexander's recent "tastelessness."

I was so comfortable with the new work that I failed to notice the ambivalent expressions on the faces of those looking at *Revolving Figure*, which was back from the Whitney show, the acrylic-glass sculpture *Spirit*, and the seventeen other sculptures composed of blatantly nontraditional art materials.

Unfortunately, the exhibition was neither a critical nor a financial success. If anything, the nineteen experimental works inspired distaste, not interest. Although occasionally exhibited, they have never been part of the market. As Dolly Perls pointed out to me in a barbed comment shortly after Alexander's death, the later work "didn't sell like hotcakes."

As the reviews attested, Alexander's more radical new constructions were at odds with what was expected. They were described as "eccentric," if not worse. Stuart Preston of *The New York Times*, who identified Archipenko as a "Cubist satellite in the heroic early days who is still going strong at the age of 70," found the sculpto-paintings "admirable" but commented that a number had "a superficial ornamentation that is frequently gaudy and distracting."[1] While he later overcame his distaste, Robert Coates, the art critic for *The New Yorker* who named the New York School the "Abstract Expressionists," described Archipenko as "garish" in his color, which he called a "failure" in taste.[2] Emily Genauer of *The Herald Tribune* described the "artsy-craftsy look" and the "ubiquitous gift-shop ware some of his pieces recall."[3]

The lack of positive response was also accorded *Repose (Cleopatra)*, my favorite piece in the show. Years later, the art historian and critic Robert Rosenblum had another look at the piece—which had reclaimed its original title, *Cleopatra*—and understood in hindsight the value of this dismissed work. In 1984, on the occasion of the Bard College exhibition *Archipenko: Drawings, Reliefs, and Constructions*, Rosenblum wrote, "From any angle, this imposing relief jarred against every preconception about what was good or bad art; but it nevertheless had the kind of grand-scale, stubborn presence that refused to go away and that could perhaps re-enter the history of art in other, more surprising ways." He also commented that *Cleopatra* is "a road blocking challenge that reshuffles the past, present, and future of what happened in 20th-century art."[4]

While I was busy admiring the new work, the collectors had gravitated to the seven small bronze statuettes which had been modeled, cast, and finished during Alexander's short summer months in Woodstock: *Walking, Lying Horizontal Figure, Who Is She?, Flying, Espanola, Dancer,* and *Gold and Black* (figs. 37 to 43). These were the only sculptures from the show that sold, as they were modest in price as well as in size.

Fig. 37 Alexander Archipenko, *Walking*, 1957, bronze, 16¹/₈ x 5³/₄ x 2 in. (40.9 x 14.6 x 5.1 cm), Frances Gray Collection

Fig. 38 Alexander Archipenko, *Lying Horizontal Figure*, 1957, bronze, 4½ x 14 in. (11.4 x 35.6 cm), private collection

Fig. 39 Alexander Archipenko, *Who Is She?*, 1957, bronze, 11¼ in. (28.5 cm), private collection >

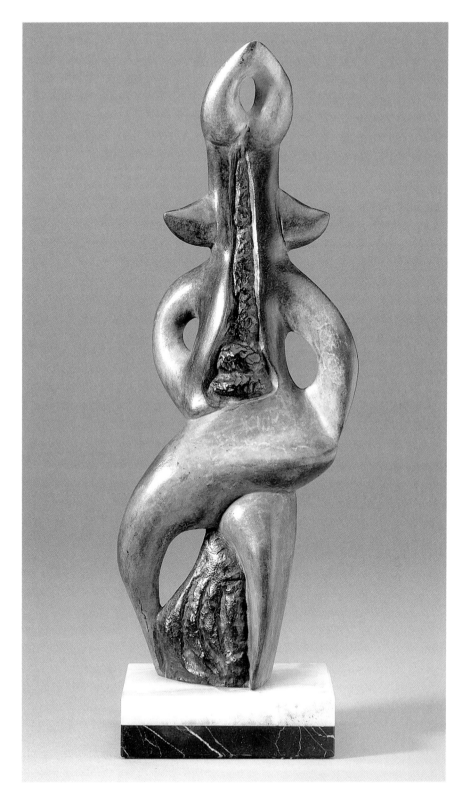

93

< Fig. 40 Alexander Archipenko, *Flying*, 1957, bronze, 11⁷/₈ x 3³/₄ x 3¹/₈ in. (30.2 x 9.5 x 7.9 cm), Frances Gray Collection

Fig. 41 Alexander Archipenko, *Espanola*, 1957, bronze, 13⁵/₈ x 4³/₄ x 2¹/₂ in. (35.6 x 12.1 x 6.4 cm), Frances Gray Collection
Fig. 42 Alexander Archipenko, *Dancer*, 1957, bronze, 12⁷/₈ x 3⁵/₈ x 2⁷/₈ in. (37.7 x 9.8 x 7.3 cm), Frances Gray Collection

Fig. 43 Alexander Archipenko, *Gold and Black*, 1957, bronze, 6½ in. (16.5 cm), private collection

What collectors and the public expected and wanted was vintage Archipenko—the familiar images, those produced in Europe when Herwarth Walden, the German entrepreneur of the international avant-garde, was his champion. These early works had been collected by art patrons such as Katherine Dreier, who bought directly from the artists, including Alexander, and often helped to sell or place them for the artists' benefit. She later gave her collection to Yale and the Guggenheim. Joseph Hirshhorn, another patron who enjoyed dealing directly with artists, also collected Archipenko's signature work from the early twentieth century. These Modernist works by Archipenko were part of art history, documented and unquestionable.

Although Alexander read the unfavorable reviews of his show, he didn't dwell on them. He was self-assured that his name in history would be there forever. With all his dark moods, Alexander never took the American critics as seriously as they took themselves. He felt he knew better. His was the broader view, that of a creative artist. In effect wearing blinders about the importance of the critical response, he just kept working—putting a great deal of effort into organizing exhibitions of his works in Europe and spending a good amount of time making crates to ship new pieces overseas.

He also had time for me. Like a sketch for one of his sculptures, I was in development. Not completely formed yet or ready to be shown, I had potential. When Alexander and I began to appear in public together, I was self-conscious and uncomfortable in a crowd, a salamander making myself invisible in a room. I was thin-skinned and vulnerable.

* * *

We were separated by a dense throng of people balancing glasses of red wine. Plastic cups littered most surfaces as people squeezed about. I could see Alexander off to one side, not particularly happy. Red wine was never his choice. The buffet was blocked off, and I was pinned in a corner next to a potted plant which had been used as an ashtray.

Our hosts, Mathilde and Fritz Low, were one of several couples who made it a point to include me in the invitations to their homes. New York always had many different social circles which mixed, and Mathilde's list included people as diverse as Saul Bellow, when he visited New York, and Virginia Zabriskie and artists from her stable. For tonight's party, the Lows had invited everyone from Peggy Guggenheim to writers from *The New Yorker*.

At first, I assumed Alexander's friends thought that I was a student he brought along. However, I soon realized that he always had a girlfriend in tow. I was the current girlfriend. Although Alexander was careful not to expose anyone to discomfort, his friends accepted this because Angelica did.

Throughout the afternoon, the Lows' apartment had absorbed people, pushing them to circulate. There were always more people invited than there were chairs. As I was trying to catch Alexander's eye, a well-dressed woman moved next to me and nodded at him. "Who's that man over there? Do you know him? I don't really know anyone here. Mathilde invited me because she gives me private lessons." With that she introduced herself and expected me to do the same.

I found myself too uncomfortable to answer. Perhaps it wasn't apparent to her, but it was to me. We were two nonentities used as fillers at Mathilde's. I was there because Mathilde and Fritz wanted Archipenko. Ironically, I was also Mathilde's student. As a trade for an Archipenko sculpture—a way of increasing her family art collection—Mathilde tried to teach me French. Never slurring the sounds, she pronounced French very distinctly. A good teacher, she used standard French literature to instruct, and, although I was not such a good student, she managed to drill some conjugations into me.

My companion nodded at Alexander again. "He looks important, but not familiar. Do you think he's an artist?"

At this point, I really wanted to leave. It was starting to feel like an awkward moment in Scarsdale.

Alexander glanced my way just before Mathilde blocked him with an introduction to someone he probably wouldn't remember. But nothing had to be said. Our rapport was on the level of eye contact rather than speech. It's through eye contact that you know you're really inside each other. Talk is superficial. Background music. Drawn to the same things, we were of the same mind when looking at Greek art at the Metropolitan or inspecting a sheet of Bakelite on Canal Street; we would both notice a tool for the studio at the same moment; and we could read each other's minds in a room full of people.

Alexander moved forward through the crush as I moved toward the foyer looking for my coat. Meeting at the elevator, we went down together and walked arm in arm out into the cool rain of Broadway and the Upper West Side.

Although I can't say that we'd fallen in love, we were rarely apart: companions headed toward a future filled with work and a commitment to one another. Every day we were bridging the difference in age, rising above the teacher-student relationship, and forming an inseparable companionship.

I wasn't concerned about losing my parents' financial support if they discovered the truth about our relationship. They were saving the cost of Yale as it was, and I paid no tuition at the Archipenko Art School. I just wanted to avoid conflict. My mother unconsciously worked hard to appear sophisticated and would have been at a loss to explain Alexander to her friends as my boyfriend. The term "lover" did not exist in my parents' vocabulary. For me to disappear out of their lives with a foreigner of a different social class would reflect poorly on them. Knowing they also wouldn't be able to comprehend that I might choose a man fifty years my senior (this had come as a surprise even to me) who was deeply bound to his wife, I kept my secret.

Then, on December 5, 1957, Angelica died.

* * *

When I arrived at the studio to help Alexander with some business correspondence, his face was sad, sinking into itself. It was obvious that he had had something to drink. He didn't have to tell me. It was apparent. The past was speeding by him, and he needed to stay in the present and keep steering. Any disappointment or reaction Alexander had over the public response to the Perls show was overshadowed by the death of his wife of thirty-six years.

His enlargement of a sculpture that she'd made to mark her burial site, which he knew would later also accommodate him, was part of the long mourning process which he chose for himself. The loss had been gradual and the prolongation was exceptionally painful for both of them. He was realistic in knowing that his own healing would take time. She was the first to go, and he honored her with a traditional Catholic funeral and an open casket. It was clear to me that the actual death was an event for which he'd been preparing for too long, and that watching her suffering come to an end was also a great relief.

My immediate location in all of this? Perhaps upstream. Although I was concerned for Alexander, in my heart I knew he would manage it all with or without me. He didn't want or need my comfort. The old friends who rallied around him offered that. I was very much out of the picture—relieved to be far away from it all, a part of his other life. In fact, I believe Alexander's Ukrainian friends knew about Angelica's death before I did. Not having been invited, I wasn't part of the funeral. This was a past with which I had no connection. If I had any feelings about Angelica's death, they were not particularly clear to me. Since I didn't attend the service, even the contagion of sadness wasn't mine. Alexander's Ukrainian friends, who took it upon themselves to be his support, would have been shocked had I been there. In fact, I would encounter the Ukrainians and their shock seven years later when, as his wife, I was preparing Alexander's funeral.

This was a sorrowful time in Alexander's life, to which I was only a partial witness. He showed me what he wanted me to see. And that was a productive, energetic person in whom there was very little room for sadness. If anything, the sadness moved him forward. He didn't want to dwell.

Work and planning were his antidote to grief just as his career was also about to undergo a radical shift in direction. The lack of public interest in the newer multi-material works thrust Archipenko into both a new frenzy of activity and a pragmatic compromise that would last for the remainder of his life.

Chapter Seven
Variants and Replicas

When I first entered the studio with the fan running on high, the smell seemed interchangeable with the New Jersey Turnpike. Once inside, it was too late. I felt damaged. The odor of acid chemicals blowtorched onto heated bronze made my eyes smart and my nostrils itch, and the studio had a noise-filled factory atmosphere. The metal and sheets of Bakelite were gone, and a thin layer of dust coated the windows and tinted Alexander's apron gray.

After the disappointing reaction to his new work at the Perls exhibition, the challenges and isolation involved with forward thinking were undeniable for Alexander. Instead of returning to his late multi-material experiments, he moved on to working more often—but not always—with forms which were more conducive to what collectors might understand, in a material they were familiar with, preferably bronze.

He was practical. Sales paid the rent, and commercial success was part of why collectors and dealers were attracted to his art. Perls's reaction to the lack of sales for the new work was also pragmatic. Perls didn't cast judgments, but just moved on and got what he needed: bronzes of Archipenko's famous signature images.

Now, with the encouragement of Perls, the formula developed. Even though many early images had not been cast in bronze because of the expense, collectors favored bronze casts of known works which had an exhibition provenance or written review that memorialized Archipenko's historical importance. Alexander began producing variants, contemporary plaster models of his famous early works—often in different sizes—which would be cast in bronze. If it meant he had to redo an old idea, he accepted that.

Alexander's practice was to use reproduced images or vintage photographs of early works—to which he no longer had access—to create new models from which he could cast a bronze edition. Technically, a variant is a reinterpretation of an earlier original model. A work might inspire any number of variants in similar or different sizes, which in turn could be replicated in different media. Historically, sculptors or their assistants since Michelangelo had produced variants.

Fig. 44 Alexander Archipenko, *Woman with Fan*, 1914, wood, sheet metal, glass bottle, metal funnel, and paint, 42½ x 24¼ x 5¼ in. (108 x 61.5 x 13.5 cm), Tel Aviv Museum of Art, Tel Aviv, Israel

Fig. 45 Alexander Archipenko, *Woman with Fan*, 1914/1962, bronze, 35½ in. (90.2 cm), Art Gallery of Hamilton, Hamilton, Ontario, Canada

Although Perls occasionally requested a specific sculpture for a client, Alexander often chose which early pieces to re-create. Against a narrow wall, adjoining the door that led into this big noisy mess of a workshop, was a tall black metal cabinet, and in it was a trove of old catalogues and monographs which dated back to his early career in Germany and France. He had also amassed both copies and original vintage photographs of works and places, arranged in chronological order to convey the essence of their specific time. These scrapbook albums traveled with him from studio to studio. Never carelessly placed around the workshop, they were carefully shelved to be looked at on a clean table once the din of the day had passed.

Alexander now organized his studios both in New York and Woodstock so he could easily oversee the final finishing of bronzes. Whenever possible he had the work semi-finished at the foundry, but he always preferred to supervise the chasing or do it himself. As usual, he found a way to make all of this interesting. As he dipped back and forth, attempting to reconstruct his past achievements, he was still discovering. Early ideas gave him new ones. When he created the second variant of the 1914 *Woman with Fan* (fig. 44), which was housed in the Tel Aviv Museum, it was from an early photograph and memory. As he transposed the original into bronze, the photograph gave him visual information he didn't have before. In the photograph of the original—which is a collage/construction of wood, sheet metal, a glass bottle, and a metal funnel—the fan is flat and raised. Recapturing details which he now noticed, his new bronze version (fig. 45) is more about moving shadows, reflection, and creating depth. This variant, in a sense, is also a memorial to the fragility of the early work. Throughout 1958, Alexander completed new editions of *Torso in Space* (fig. 46), *Flat Torso* (fig. 17), *Woman Combing Her Hair* (fig. 52), *Seated Woman Combing Her Hair, Green Concave, Standing Woman, Still Life and Vase, Woman with Fan, Black Concave*, and *Seated Geometric Figure*. By the time Alexander had his next exhibition with Perls in 1959, the show would be exclusively bronzes—over half of which were dated between 1909 and 1921. Archipenko was the master of leaps in time.

With Alexander's focus obviously back on his more familiar style, Perls eagerly planned another Archipenko show. He had collectors who understood the value of a historically known artist and the durable value of bronze. For his part, Alexander was grateful to be working with Perls. When the gallery owner bought something himself or sold an Archipenko to a buyer, he paid Alexander immediately. Perls also sold and consigned to other dealers who had additional reservoirs of clients in various locations.

In May 1958, Alexander signed a formal contract with Eric Estorick. In the agreement, Estorick claimed exclusive rights as Alexander's dealer in England and Switzerland and promised a "large exhibition and sale" of Alexander's work in an "important gallery or

Fig. 46 Alexander Archipenko, *Torso in Space*, 1935, bronze, $8^7/_8$ x $26^7/_8$ x 6 in. (22.5 x 68.3 x 15.2 cm),
Museum of Fine Arts, Houston, TX

museum" by 1960.[1] The carrot before Alexander's nose was an exhibition at the Tate. The agreement also allowed Estorick to take seventeen works—including three sculpto-paintings—to London "for trial" before the exhibit was confirmed. Writing Alexander a check on account for $2,500 against future sales, Estorick left for England with half of the seventeen works. Nine bronzes "were to follow almost immediately." Estorick wanted the bronzes to secure the show and put Archipenko "back in the picture." During the negotiations, Estorick and Archipenko also decided on a price for limited edition castings of *Geometric Statuette* (fig. 22).

Although all this activity was comforting in those lean years, Perls's proposed bronze show and any London exhibit were in the future. During the year after Angelica's death, Alexander continued his frugal, work-centered routine. He was able to mourn profoundly and yet participate with no disruption in daily life, which included his "other life" with me. As was true from our first summer together, Alexander did not seem conflicted feeling many ways at once. Initially, Angelica's death didn't seem to change our relationship. Although Alexander was now living in the apartment alone, I still spent nights with my parents or grandparents.

* * *

The first time I entered Alexander's apartment in the months after Angelica's death, it felt abandoned and forlorn. With its stop-gap furnishings, pieces of odd fabrics draping the windows, and secondhand lamps and end tables, it gave off the aura of a temporary solution. With a fire escape, the modest apartment on 19th Street was vintage New York, the same type *The Honeymooners* had on television. The parquet floors were bare, clean but worn down. The linoleum in the kitchen was uneven and grimy in the corners. The windows looked out back on the neighbors' fire escapes and shaded windows. While the rest of the apartment had been occupied by Angelica and her health aide, Alexander had lived in a tiny space the size of a child's or maid's room—similar dimensions to my room at my parents' Scarsdale apartment. If I did find myself staying at Alexander's apartment, I never brought clothes or personal belongings.

The only place we actually lived together in the immediate post-Angelica period was Woodstock, in the summer of 1958. Camping out in the studio progressed to a semi-domestic arrangement which even included pets. I don't remember the names of the birds, only that the memory of befriending a black crow and keeping it as a companion when he was a child in Kiev was active in Alexander's mind when we visited a pet store at the beginning of summer and returned with two parakeets.

These two little birds were attractive until you owned them. Alexander wanted them to be my feathered friends. Imagining I could teach them to say things, he encouraged me to tempt them onto my finger. Unfortunately, the one that did perch got scolded by the one that was resistant, and I was forced to witness one parakeet abusing the other as I tried to get my hand out of the cage before blood was drawn. It was easy for me to imagine a brutal bird battle as a result of my training session.

Insisting the two birds have fresh air, Alexander installed their cage in a tree in the small garden adjacent to his studio. This was not a typical garden, although it did have some tiger lilies and wild roses nestled against the rock wall. Alexander's understanding of bird psychology was limited. In the humid heat of the summer he put up an awning and used this space as an extension of his workshop, power tools and all. Much of his bronze finishing went on there, and the sounds and smells of a blowtorch on acid made even the outdoor air feel close. Inside the studio, typing in the late afternoon, I would hear intermittent bird shrieks above the sound of his grinding machines as he continued to do the finish work on his bronze statues.

Although Alexander had no solo shows in 1958, he was represented in at least sixteen different exhibitions. His work was seen in the context of established galleries in Paris and London and in important exhibitions in museums in New York, Duisburg, Stockholm, and Brussels. The next Perls show was scheduled for October 1959. The major London show had yet to materialize.

Almost immediately after Archipenko and Estorick had signed the agreement of May 12, 1958, both dealer and artist had begun retreating from the arrangement. By mid-June, they were exchanging accusations and implied threats. In their correspondence that summer, Estorick avoided responding to Alexander's requested confirmation of the date and venue of this "large" show. For his part, Alexander kept claiming that the rest of the "trial" works were "just going to the foundry" or "on their way," but he never sent them. It's clear from the letters that Estorick's equivocations frustrated Alexander, who appears to have been holding the bronzes hostage until Estorick produced a confirmation from the Tate or another reputable gallery. Because of the prohibitive cost of bronze casting, it's possible that Alexander never even sent the disputed models to the foundry. The conflict escalated as Estorick pressed Alexander for the "anxiously awaited" missing bronzes, and, on August 22, Alexander rescinded Estorick's rights as his dealer beyond a London exhibit.

Behind the scenes, both were attempting to involve Perls. As Archipenko's art dealer in New York, Perls took the position that whoever dealt with Archipenko outside his dealership was on his own. Although Perls might introduce potential dealers such as Estorick, he made it clear that he wouldn't intervene if there was a misunderstanding. Alexander was left to deal with Estorick on his own.

I knew nothing of this growing controversy, as I was busy that summer preparing for my first exhibit. Still focused on my future, Alexander had arranged a one-person show for me at a gallery on Madison Avenue. He had decided that the Delacorte Gallery—in a brownstone just doors down from the Perls Galleries—was an optimum location for my first exhibit. Because Delacorte was young and interested in the aesthetics of ethnic art, Alexander saw him as a good connection for me. Earlier in the year we'd seen a modest exhibit of Egyptian Coptic textiles and then a show of Aborigine Australian bark paintings installed in this out-of-the-way gallery. The venue was very fresh, bringing forth inspirational works from exotic places as well as affordable works an artist could collect.

Not discouraged by the fact that Delacorte didn't show contemporary artists, Alexander posed his question to the enterprising young gallerist. "Frances is doing sculpture. Would you be interested in showing her work?" The proposal was only plausible because Alexander was who he was.

As I completed a series of carvings and bas-reliefs for my exhibit, I often had difficulty concentrating. Every time the parakeets shrieked, I was sure a snake was entering their cage. Garden snakes were everywhere, leaving their skins on rocks. In all of this, Alexander was my opposite; he never seemed to worry. Perhaps he was even oblivious to the birds' signs of distress.

Once we were back in the city that fall, Alexander began moving things around. Angelica's presence was slowly leaving the apartment. We still lived and worked separately, however. Closing the school in the fall of 1958, Alexander had moved from the Lincoln Arcade Building to a rented commercial loft at 143 West 20th Street, and I finally moved into my own place, a live-in studio on 56th Street and Eighth Avenue. No more tiny maid's room, no more commutes from Scarsdale. It was pure freedom, with joy thrown in for good measure.

* * *

When Alexander rang the doorbell, I peeked out with the door's safety latch still fastened. It was an odd time for him to visit without letting me know he was on his way. It was, however, the first time I would actually be sleeping alone in New York City. Alone except for the parakeets, that is. I hadn't been able to abandon them to Alexander.

My first studio/home was in another old New York artists' building, in walking distance from Carnegie Hall. Although I'd rented it as a workspace, I lived there with a hot plate and a cot. With its high metal ceiling and big studio windows letting in the noisy traffic from Eighth Avenue, I would be living marginally, without a refrigerator and with the toilet and shower a walk away in the communal bathroom that was kept quite clean by the janitor. There was one other live-in tenant on the floor, a hunched-over seamstress who had seen better days, which she loved to talk about.

I had found the space through one of Alexander's longtime friends and former students, who had a studio on the same floor. She worked there most days, her boxer in silent attendance. I was impressed by the dog, a lean and athletic animal that walked by her side and sat at her feet. So was Alexander.

With a huge grin on his face when I opened the door, Alexander held up a cardboard box with a little Dalmatian puppy spilling over the edge. My new building came with a different type of danger than the Lincoln Arcade, and Alexander was convinced that I needed my own canine companion. The glass door that led to the elevator was on the street bordering the Hell's Kitchen neighborhood, with its odors of food and booze. There was a real possibility of being mugged in the unattended elevator at night. Because many of the studios were used for rehearsals, there was always traffic in and out going to all the floors. More than once, I heard the elevator alarm ring during the night and looked out my window to see a police car pull up in front of the building.

Alexander presented my guard dog to me like a work of art. Her nose looked like licorice, and her eyes seemed to be made–up with black eyeliner. Sappho, whom he'd already named, was packed in shredded newspaper, a study in black and white. We were amazed at her prettiness and sweet shyness. I'd never had a dog, much less a puppy, so it was all a very exciting surprise. When she jumped out of the box into my arms, snuggling against me and licking me as if I were her new mother, we bonded. Alexander was still grinning. We found an old sock for her to pull on and took turns engaging her in a tug of war. Before long, exhausted and overstressed, the puppy found a hidden corner.

The parakeets were out of their cage, fluttering around and calling out taunts. The cage had its own stand near the window, but I hated the idea of a bird in captivity and always let them loose in the room. They flew around, pecking away at the plaster ceiling cornices and spewing bird seed on the floor.

I remain grateful to Alexander for introducing me to the pleasure of owning pets. Every day was enjoyable as Sappho and I had marvelous walks in Central Park. On the other hand, I was now on a very tight budget with three pets to feed—the Dalmatian puppy and two raucous parakeets. A loaf of sliced bread, peanut butter, oatmeal, skim-milk powder, raisins, apples, and canned food were my staples. Frequently, I was down to the peanut butter. Since juggling numbers was never my forte, I didn't budget or bargain shop. I just tried to keep a step ahead without hoarding. The most important item was dog food; usually I had an extra bag on hand.

Moving into a workspace that could double as a residence was the equivalent of getting a diploma into the grown-up world. My time was my own. I could sleep or not sleep, prepare my own meals to eat or not eat. In other words, I was now definitely in charge—or at least in charge of myself. Having my own home felt like a new beginning, as well as a trial separation from my past. My self-determination would be tested.

And how did Alexander fit into all of this? Because my studio was so small, especially with the animals he'd given me, Alexander never spent the night there. However, we met up every evening, Sappho and I often staying over at his apartment. It didn't seem to matter where we were living or how often I actually saw Alexander. We were committed. He seemed happy and playful again, and I felt his sadness over Angelica lifting.

Alexander's arrival with the puppy was also the beginning of a new self-awareness for me. I was given a dependent by the person who on some level held me dependent. It was all mixed up with a false sense of promised protection. Was I a stray? Or was I still a dependent? His gift of Sappho increased my puzzlement. But, for me, our connection felt permanent. On every level, I could not imagine my life without this person.

I marveled every day at the natural electricity that fueled the artist and the man. Nothing discouraged him. Not ever-looming financial ruin; the apparent collusion of art dealers and museum directors; an art world which now typecast him as "Cubist" and rejected his work as "decorative" or "mannerist" in favor of new trends; the grueling mental and physical toll it took to represent himself and mount his own shows; or the long-term illness and death of his beloved wife. Always transcending the background noise of his chaotic life, he never looked back. Rejection, loss, betrayal, and disappointment were no match for the resources on which Archipenko drew. Never revealing that he was desperate for money, if he saw an opportunity—as with the variants—he moved toward it, whether abroad or at home. Despite his cynical side, he was basically optimistic, managing to live without pessimism or fear, simply embracing and accepting what he had. He didn't suffer from anxiety as most people do.

As we neared the one-year anniversary of Angelica's death, Alexander slowly made his apartment his own, and Sappho and I spent more nights with him there. Although Alexander occasionally woke from sleep, still hearing Angelica's bell calling him, the part of him which was very private and would always belong to her eventually came to be at peace with itself. And I had a new role in Alexander's life: that of eyewitness.

Chapter Eight
Emotions and Compromises

Eric Estorick appeared at the door of his room after we were signaled up from the lobby of the four-star hotel on Madison Avenue, just a few blocks away from the Perls Galleries where we'd been visiting. The room was dim, all the curtains were drawn, and Estorick was wearing a black silk dressing gown, which, to my eyes, appeared dark and creepy. Was this a sophisticated person or just someone arising from a decadent evening? I was surprised that he was not fully dressed, since Alexander was wearing a tie, his habit of dress when outside of his studio/workshop.

"Come in, good to see you. Who's this you have with you?" When Estorick glanced at me, I had the sensation of being looked over and dismissed. Clearly, I was irrelevant. I felt intimidation, if not disrespect.

Alexander's voice was low and contained. "My friend Frances will take notes, so that there'll be no misunderstanding."

Alexander hadn't briefed me, and only much later did I learn the full extent of the complicated game they were playing. In mid-October, because Estorick had yet to confirm a London show, Alexander wrote to Estorick canceling that plan. In return mail dated October 20, 1958, Estorick described himself as "aghast" at the news, claiming he had been in "discussions" with the O'Hana Gallery and with officials from the Arts Council and the British Council about the Archipenko exhibit and thus, "I certainly cannot sit back and passively accept your request to not continue any further arrangements for the year of 1960." Reiterating, "I must have all the work to help me prepare this big exhibition. . . . From June 18th I have been waiting and not a single additional work has arrived," Estorick ends with a letter suggesting they meet in New York.[1]

The fires had been further fanned by the intervention of Erica Brausen of the Hanover Gallery, from whom Alexander had just received a letter claiming that she'd witnessed bronzes being made "of three of your works on the instructions of a certain gentlemen in London."[2] She later identified Estorick and *Geometric Statuette* (fig. 22).

The May 12 contract had given Estorick the "exclusive" right to "order" from Archipenko "any extra copy or cast of each sculpture" with Alexander's signature. It is clear from his letters, however, that Alexander signed the agreement with the understanding that any bronze edition of a plaster held by Estorick would be cast in New York under Alexander's supervision. When Brausen asked whether Alexander knew about or gave permission for this casting of his work by a London foundry, Alexander wrote back thanking her and asking for her help to "defend my name and my interest in England."

Now Alexander was defending his name in person. He stayed focused and calm. "Perls suggested that you wanted to see me. So, here I am. I think we have a few things to talk about before you return to London."

Estorick picked up a coffee cup from his room service tray and took a sip. "So. Why are you slow in casting the works that you promised?"

I could tell by the deepening frown on Alexander's brow that a disturbance might surface, but he remained calm. "The foundry is always slow."

Estorick set his cup down a bit too forcefully. "I can't keep postponing."

Like a pitcher at a baseball game, Estorick began issuing confusing signals. "And just so you know, I'm still in negotiation with the Tate, and after your exhibition in my gallery, they'll be able to plan more precisely what they want to exhibit. But I need the rest of the work."

When Alexander rose to leave, Estorick changed directions once again and said he was "interested in purchasing" the consigned bronzes himself.

With nothing resolved, they parted but met again in December, and this time, Estorick surprised Archipenko by producing three bronze statues of *Geometric Statuette*. Instead of bringing the plaster to New York to honor Alexander's expectation that the contract gave him the right to supervise the bronze castings himself, Estorick had had them cast at a London foundry. He had been wily in the wording of their agreement. The contract Alexander signed had not specifically prohibited the bronzes from being fabricated without Archipenko's oversight, and Estorick had gone ahead on his own.

Alexander remained calm, however. He was being paid. A handwritten invoice on Hotel Adams stationery records the transaction: "The edition of 3 bronzes of my statue "Geometric Figure 1914) [sic] cast by Mr. Estorick in London. Price for 3 copy $1.800. Sold. Dec. 20 1958 to Mr. Estorik [sic]. A. Archipenko."[3]

Money in this instance was Alexander's priority, and he forced himself to assume the best outcome. In fact, Alexander signed an additional agreement to supervise three more bronze casts of *Geometric Statuette* for another $1,800. Alexander may have been disturbed by Estorick's disregard, but he didn't want to miss an opportunity to make a profit. With continuing concerns about how bronze casts were actually being fabricated, Alexander no longer had any quality control.

As 1958 came to a close, a short-lived détente settled over these two stubborn personalities. The London show was not mentioned again in their correspondence. Instead, Alexander turned his focus to another exhibit, this one opening back in New York. Mine.

* * *

It had been thrilling to be working for a show, alone in my own studio with Sappho at my feet. While I did the larger bas-reliefs and wood carving in Woodstock, I completed drawings and sculptures in bronze and aluminum in my new space on 56th Street. However, now that the date at the Delacorte was set and all the logistics were in place, the exhibition began to feel inevitable. As the show neared, I tried to maintain a realistic attitude, but its underpinnings were a forced optimism. It was not that I wasn't worthy, or that the work would do better ignored. I just felt an undercurrent of strangeness which was like a case of the hives, relentless. My anticipation of the aftermath was even more confusing. The idea of promotion and sales was far removed from my intent when I actually worked at my art.

Excited about my coming show, my mother invited her friends, and my father generously planned to print the catalogue with his company's offset press. In my heart, however, I knew it was a stretch for my parents and their friends to understand my work or the work of my teacher. My parents wanted to support me, of course. They were proud of me. They wouldn't be proud, however, if they were forced to confront the truth about my relationship—now in its fourth year—with my teacher.

By the day of the actual opening in January 1959, I was giddy with unease. I arrived with makeup in place, wearing a simple navy sleeveless sheath with a string of pearls I had received as a present for my sixteenth birthday. The gallery, a few steps below ground level on fashionable Madison Avenue, was installed with my small castings—some in aluminum and polychromed—on pedestals tastefully lit and comfortably spaced. White wine and cheese were set up in the back gallery.

When no one had arrived yet, I walked around the block and sat on a bench outside Central Park. The opening felt exaggerated and more than I was ready for. I wasn't a careerist. I was less than fully committed. I wasn't associating with artists of my age. The only other artist I saw was Alexander. And this would, of course, be one of the rare occasions when my parents were in the same room as Alexander and me. If they suspected anything, they would know more than they wanted to and would have to collude with me so that everyone could live with their lies. Deception works both ways.

Because they wouldn't want to see my real relationship with Alexander, they'd work even harder than I to cover it up.

The issue was really my competency in keeping my secret. I had to make sure they had no reason to be suspicious—and not because I'd be embarrassed or ashamed if they found out. Their ultimate anger wouldn't come from my deception or my choice of a mate, but from the fact that I was an incompetent liar, and in that way an embarrassment to them socially. I had nothing to fear except the possibility of accidentally forcing their hand with overt proof.

By the time I returned to the gallery, my parents had arrived and were greeting Alexander, who'd worn a suit, tie, and clean white shirt for the event. They even fussed a bit over my mentor, thanking him for taking such an interest in his student. Alexander glanced up and caught my eye. That was enough for me.

Clothed in something smart in gray with silver jewelry, which she had bought on a trip to Acapulco, my mother began circulating and greeting the people she'd invited. Handing out the catalogues he'd printed, my father was also busy showing visitors around. To me it felt like a funeral, where everyone is polite but reserved and anxious to leave. Although the show sold sparingly, my parents were proud. Maybe I hadn't landed a respectable husband, but I was doing something acceptably interesting.

Even more proud was Alexander. I understood, however, that my art had only been accepted for shows in New York (and later in Europe) because of my connection to him. When my exhibit was reviewed as "semi-abstract and inscrutable" and "indebted to her teacher," I accepted that. Although my work was good—not just school pieces—it wasn't mature. That my work had been recommended by Alexander Archipenko was what counted. And he had faith in me.

I was accepting life as it was developing for me. Despite my mother's efforts, I hadn't completed four years of college and settled in the suburbs. At the age of twenty-two, I was living a life vastly different from my parent's notion of a woman's comfortable role in society.

Immediately after my opening at the Delacorte, Alexander left for Europe to arrange shows for both of us. His first stop, however, was London. Alexander had learned that Estorick was continuing to cast his work. When Alexander confirmed this with the owner of the foundry, he confronted Estorick. In a letter to me dated January 19, 1959, Alexander wrote, "I told Estorick I quit business with him. Tomorrow he's supposed to pay for five casted bronzes to buy from the work he brought from New York and . . . to return [the rest] to me. He is surprised and apparently regrets."[4]

By the next morning, Alexander took a more pragmatic view, signing a new agreement on January 20, 1959, which gave Estorick—whom he had fired just the day before—even more rights. Although Estorick didn't pay Alexander at that meeting, in the new written agreement he committed to paying for all or some of the ten works he had brought with him from New York, returning the balance he didn't buy.

Surprisingly, at this meeting, Estorick then showed Alexander "three casts of polychrome terra-cotta" which he asked Alexander to finish in polychrome and sign. Their agreement also obligated Alexander to polychrome two bronzes from 1915 and four others which Estorick himself had already cast in London. These, according to their new contract, would be delivered to Archipenko for coloring for a fee of another $4,200. Estorick included the stipulation that Alexander not "duplicate" any of the bronzes he was sending for coloring. The agreement further confirmed that Archipenko "approved" the three disputed bronzes of *Geometric Statuette* cast by Estorick "as finished." Alexander then gave Estorick the rights to three more copies: an "exclusive series of six bronzes of the *Geometric* figure of 1913/14, of which three copies were cast by me [Estorick]." The final page of the agreement reiterates the price for *Geometric Statuette*: $700 each.[5]

In a postcard sent to me from Paris, Alexander wrote: "Estorick has a terrible reputation here." But when Alexander returned to New York, he was still doing business with the London dealer.

Now that Alexander no longer needed tuition from paying students, in the summer of 1959 we moved into the main house at the school in Woodstock, where we lived together and continued to develop as a couple—with all the emotions and compromises that entails.

Chapter Nine
Turning Point

The smell of mothballs when we arrived at Woodstock was reassuring. I can still feel the yellowed newspaper which we gathered off the mattresses, the dampness dispersing as the boards came off the windows and we opened the house to the summer sunshine. As he did each summer, Alexander repaired water damage from the winter while I spent time and baking soda trying to sanitize the hopeless old fridge. Alexander always hated to see me cleaning or scrubbing. It didn't fit with the pedestal he imagined me on. But I was determined. I couldn't get the odor in the old refrigerator up to my standards. It had been left too many winter months turned off—and too many summer months with spills. Finally, we settled in and prepared to entertain our first houseguests as a couple.

When Alexander woke before I did and started the coffee in the school's kitchen, he also began his daily routine of scraping fresh garlic on his morning toast. This folk remedy for longevity didn't usually lose its pungent effect until evening. That it had an antisocial edge was usually no issue for me, as long as it wasn't obviously offensive. Garlic in an enclosed vehicle had that possibility. I'd been looking forward to our hosting friends together as a new adventure. While I was still outgrowing my shyness, I was also feeling my new status. Helena and her husband John had entertained us many times in their apartment on Riverside Drive, where Helena's Polish accent and attempts at French cooking always created a charming evening for Alexander to bask in a European ambiance. It was our turn to thank them, and the pungent smell of garlic so early in the morning didn't seem fair to share in a ratty car with guests at the beginning of the weekend, even for a short ride. My thoughts went to Angelica, dead but not forgotten by me. She knew what she was talking about when she called Alexander "a peasant."

As we headed to town to pick up our visitors from the bus, the smell of Alexander's breath turned me into a shrew. "Sappho should sit next to you; just stay away from me."

"Frances, this is no problem." His reply was meant to reassure.

I thought it was a problem. When I jumped out of the car to greet our friends, I was still agitated. Of course, garlic wasn't the real problem. The deeper issue was that I had asked him to forgo garlic for the day, politely explaining the reasons for my request. I had assumed he agreed with me. Instead, he acted as if he hadn't heard me. I felt dismissed, and so I lashed out.

As it happened, all of Helena's "Polish countess" facade, enhanced by her accent, hid her country peasant stock. She probably even enjoyed Alexander's smell. John was oblivious and soon disappeared for long walks in the woods, following Sappho's tracks.

In reflecting on this incident many years later, I asked myself why the event was still so potent in my imagination. Certainly the smell couldn't linger that long. However, the emotional turning point that it represented could. That day, I confronted the reality that I wanted to control Alexander and couldn't. My feelings at the moment were intense, and it was easier to blame the smell of garlic than the unconscious will of my "partner." He was a strong free spirit, and the garlic definitely symbolized that.

In this incident there was the intimation that I had also lost control of my life if I couldn't control him. Here I was on the brink of permanent attachment to a man who'd dismissed my request as if it were a whim. Could I trust him to value my interests? Did I want anything for myself anymore? What did I even want?

Because I was unprepared to acknowledge the lack of control over my life that was part of our arrangement, the smell of garlic was my cover. Even if I'd realized the stakes at the time, I wasn't ready to face my loss of control and independence. Instead, I told

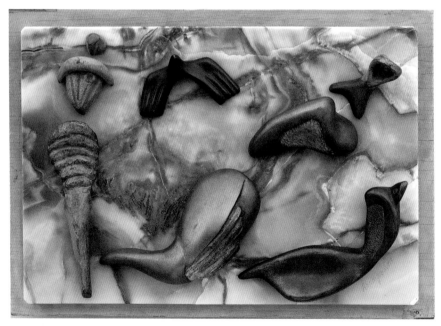

Fig. 47 Alexander Archipenko, *Eagle*, 1959, bronze and marble, 10½ x 15½ x ¾ in. (26.7 x 39.4 x 2 cm), Frances Gray Collection

Fig. 48 Alexander Archipenko, *Abstraction*, 1959, bronze, 18³/₈ x 18¹/₂ x 4¹/₂ in. (46.7 x 47 x 11.4 cm), Frances Gray Collection
Fig. 49 Alexander Archipenko, *Seated Figure*, 1913, lithograph, framed acrylic glass, 11 x 8¹/₂ in. (28. x 21.5 cm), Frances Gray Collection

myself that the smell of garlic had fired me up, and I was defending my innocent guests. But our guests didn't need my protection. This was especially true of Alexander's Ukrainian friends. I had even less control over Alexander when they visited a few weeks later.

I heard them before I saw them. I was under the butternut tree, covered with marble dust and laboring away on my carving, when they arrived unannounced from nearby Kerhonkson, a Ukrainian vacation destination. There were two full cars which even included two young children, little boys in shorts, well groomed in a European manner. One was held in tow by his mother, Maruska Sumyk, the only woman in the group. The other child, a bit older and more on the loose, belonged to Dr. Wozniak. They had either not called in advance or Alexander had forgotten about their visit.

Inside the studio, with its high windows and thick door, the tool sounds and Alexander's concentration blocked everything else out. In addition to variants, Alexander was completing some entirely new work for the coming bronze show at the Perls Galleries. In his relief *Eagle* (fig. 47), he used marble as a background, creating a cloud-like atmosphere in which the bronze parts floated, unanchored. He was also working on a bronze relief mounted on black marble, entitled *Abstraction* (fig. 48). Inspired by his earlier work, this was a media variant of a 1913 lithograph that had been published in the Italian Futurist journal *Lacerba* (fig. 49).

Although Alexander wasn't responding to their calls, the Ukrainian party knew he was there and kept knocking until the tool stopped spinning. When Alexander finally opened the door, he didn't invite them in. Wiping his hands on his apron, he simply said, "I didn't hear you. So sorry to keep you waiting."

As usual, they were effusive: "Maestro, maestro, we would wait forever. . ."

Because the afternoon heat was steaming and the wasps were out, Alexander herded them through the school to the kitchen, where they deposited bags of food and drink on a table. They ate Polish sausage with tiny pickled mushrooms, and vodka disappeared as if it were water, without ice. Small shots of vodka were used to toast all around. They drank endlessly and, with heavy accents, tried ever more energetically to speak in English out of respect for Alexander's lack of fluency in Ukrainian. As usual, the conversation went nowhere as Alexander was prized and cheered. Part of their ritual seemed to be toasting that led to boasting, which in this case was all about Alexander.

Fig. 50 Alexander Archipenko, *Statuette*, 1915, terra-cotta, 11¾ in. (30 cm), private collection, United Kingdom

Archipenko-worshipping Ukrainians were the closest thing to family that Alexander would find, and they expected only that he be their hero. He was a Ukrainian with international respect. Although they weren't exactly his source of income, they did supplement it, and at times this was more than reassuring—it could be a helpful part of his survival. They flattered him, brought him comfort food and drink, and had limited social expectations as long as they could worship him.

Eventually, as the group got louder in its attempts to keep Alexander's attention, his thoughts began drifting. Finally he disappeared. He simply walked out of the kitchen, went back to his studio, and locked himself in. He had a deadline. Furthermore, a letter had just arrived from London. When Alexander learned that summer that the other plaster Estorick was casting from—*Statuette* (fig. 50)—didn't belong to him, the battle became bloody.

In early June, 1959, Alexander shut down Estorick's activities at the foundry. In a letter designed to sound like an inquiry, Alexander slyly blew the whistle on Estorick to the son who was apparently in charge of the family collection, Andrew Goeritz:

> Mr. Estorick informed me that he received from you some of my work which you own and made 3 castings of each one. He also wants to make more castings of these statues. We signed an agreement in which he promised not to cast any of my work again, unless the cast would be done by me personally and would be paid by him to me. You will probably understand fully how disagreeable this is from me [sic] to have him make castings for commercial purposes, all the more since it is without my permission. I would like to know if you gave him permission to do these castings, or whether he is doing it on his own initiative. Please be good enough to let me know in order for me to take further steps.[1]

On July 7, 1959, Alexander supplied Goeritz with requested specifics, including details about the casting in London "of my old work from your collection." Archipenko continues:

> We signed an agreement in which he promised not to cast any of my work again, unless the cast would be done by me personally and would be paid by him to me. At this time he persuaded me that my original belonged to him. But from another source I learned that this work is from your collection. Naturally I feel that I have no right to do casts of work which is no longer my property. Just as well did he have no right to cast work which was not his property. I see the necessity to defend my interest and for this reason I am writing to you.[2]

In his reply, Goeritz confirmed Alexander's suspicions: "I had never authorized the making of these bronze copies and Mr. Estorick proceeded to have them cast in the belief that I would be willing to part with the original and that he would be able to incorporate it into his collection."[3] Goeritz added that Estorick was instructed to turn over all copies he'd cast from the family's collection.

While Alexander was now locked in his studio, dealing with correspondence and chasing bronze statues, I was left with the Ukrainian party and didn't know what to do, since they were expecting him to return. As I was now invisible to them, they also stopped attempting to speak in English. I could have just left as Alexander had, and he would have probably not noticed or made a comment. It was natural for him to behave this way. I was a victim of my middle-class upbringing—too self-demeaning and accommodating. Alexander was all in favor of my growing out of that mode, which was one of his more endearing qualities.

Fortunately, Maruska Sumyk was a force of nature who instinctively knew how to direct a group of people and understood when it was time to leave. When the vodka was gone, Maruska cleaned the table and packed what was left in the refrigerator, leaving an untouched cheesecake which she had made especially for Alexander wrapped in a Ukrainian handkerchief for him to find. With that, she grabbed her son and headed for their car. Everyone followed. The event was over as briskly as it had begun. Until the next time, when, as had become very clear, the only person I would have control over would be myself.

When the opportunity arrived to escape to the ocean for a few days, I took it.

* * *

As Alexander drove me to the bus (he had finally reinstated his license), I felt a surge of internal heat in the anticipation of leaving. It was reminiscent of the sparks of feeling I sometimes had when leaving Scarsdale on the commuter train to go off to New York on a Saturday, or the "footloose and fancy free" feeling I'd had sitting next to my father as he drove down West Side Highway, taking me to school.

Alexander seemed emotional, almost tearful. After accepting the invitation to stay at my friend's summer rental in Provincetown, Massachusetts, I realized that Alexander had mixed feelings about my going. Displaying a rare streak of possessiveness, he might have imagined a restlessness was leading me away. In one of our more memorable conversations, he'd told me, "I find all women possible to seduce; that's why I worry about you." His own past created the insecurity that I might have a wild side too.

Shifting the gears on the rickety blue Nash station wagon, he was silent. Not that he was ever really talkative, but this silence was different—too still. Something was up. I felt that I was supposed to say something, but my mouth was dry. I said nothing. Finally, in a tone that was quite soft, Alexander said goodbye and added, in his deep voice, "I hope you'll be careful and enjoy the ocean."

Although I was happy for a breath of fresh sea air, after a few days I missed Alexander and couldn't wait to get home. I belonged with him. He was home.

As my bus drew up in front of the News Shop in Woodstock, I saw Alexander before he saw me. He was standing by the car, which was illegally parked in front of the church on the Village Green. When he saw me step off the bus, his face filled with relief and pleasure. He was so relieved I had returned, that he had a gift waiting for me: a new refrigerator, free of the smells I had been unable to remove from the old one. As the old Nash bumped down the long gravel driveway back home to the school, Alexander reached over and took my hand.

* * *

The freshly painted pedestals had been brought up from the basement, the gallery walls were spotless, the wooden floors buffed to a glow, and the lighting adjusted just so. Shoulders set back, hair in place, Alexander presented himself with a gracious and genuine smile at the launch of his bronze show at Perls Galleries on September 29, 1959 (fig. 51).

Although it was in a tasteful setting and Alexander was excited to see his works in bronze, the installation was uninspired. Even the title "Alexander Archipenko: Bronzes" on the catalogue and announcements implied objects for sale, a trophy show. Instinctively, Alexander knew that Perls, like Estorick, was primarily an opportunist. But this in no way discouraged Alexander from participating in a show from which they both expected to profit. The works, most of them variants of his well-known early sculptures, were clearly products to be sold. Alexander had no other expectations. Klaus and Dolly Perls had no other wishes. That was the way it was in 1959. Archipenko's name still reverberated from his European years and early fame in Germany—which had made it plausible for Klaus Perls to latch on. Perls was a dealer with a well-oiled sales pitch. And it worked.

Fig. 51 Perls Galleries installation view, 1959, Archipenko Foundation, Bearsville, NY

The exhibition was a critical and commercial success, and it preceded a long series of further opportunities. After a positive review in *The New Yorker* and a number of additional flattering reviews, the show sparked collectors' interest. Archipenko's work was featured prominently in the Hirshhorn sculpture show which began in 1959, circulating to eight museums and finishing its tour in Toronto. In October of that same year, Archipenko was awarded the Medaglia d'Oro at the XIII Biennale d'Arte Trivenata, an international festival of the arts in Padua, Italy. Adding to the action, Alexander was scheduled for a major retrospective in Rome and then Milan in 1963. One month after the 1959 Perls show opened, he was invited by Ernesto F. Blohm on behalf of the Asociación Cultural Humboldt to give a talk in Caracas on the occasion of the *Expresionismo en Alemania,* where several of Archipenko's pieces would be on exhibit. Blohm's invitation was confirmation that Alexander's work was probably a good investment and that his work was selling to the upper crust of international collectors.

I was having an uneasy reaction to Alexander's rising stock in the art market. The 1959 Perls opening, like most, was a social event in New York's Upper East Side which fed a snobbishness which wasn't always about art. Yes, the bronze show and its effect represented a financial comeback for Alexander, but the venue was completely counter to what I imagined his originality deserved: a curated show.

In this setting, Alexander adopted a formality which was another part of his persona. Experience had validated the truth that without sales there was no independence. He had no complaints. His works were being presented as precious. Graciously, he accepted the gallery setting as a way station for his work. But it bothered me that he was not in his usual work mode and that he had to endure people assessing his art.

Dolly Perls, wearing her usual custom shift and decked out in an oversize Calder necklace, worked the back gallery as Klaus stayed close to the entrance, catching people on their way in and out. Discreetly hidden in his left hand was a clicker that allowed him to keep count of the number of people who entered. His right hand was used to shake hands with collectors.

What fell to Perls at this show was the challenge of intelligently explaining to clients the practice of creating variants of early signature works. Of the thirty-four bronzes Perls mounted, sixteen were dated between 1909 and 1921. As Katherine Michaelsen pointed out in her article about the Archipenko/Barr conflict, "Whether a bronze edition derives from the original model or a later version of it, did not concern Perls any more than it did Archipenko."[4] However, Perls had to find a way to explain that the bronzes Archipenko had created for the show were actually later variants of early conceptions—and he had to do this without risking losing a sale. The current practice also included bronze casts being declared in editions to ensure the rarity factor, which in turn added to the investment component for the collector. Neither the various dealers nor the artist himself were necessarily consistent in their explanations or clear in their terminology.

However, Perls pumped himself up as an expert and connoisseur who tolerated Archipenko's later works in order to bring forth the early, historically important works. Since he was the president of the Art Dealers Association, Perls's opinion was valued by the art world of curators, collectors, auction houses, and other dealers. A Perls provenance was as good as it gets; that he would not be questioned surprised no one.

Perls himself might have been surprised if he'd investigated the provenance of the 1915 signature piece *Woman Combing Her Hair* (fig. 52), which he was pleased to have as a bronze edition to sell from his gallery. I doubt if he or his clients knew of the origin of this "original cast by the artist," although Perls could have easily taken the trouble to compare the bronze to the one in the museum shop at MoMA. With Alexander's permission, the Museum of Modern Art had done a replica of *Woman Combing Her Hair* from one in their collection in order to create an affordable unlimited edition of the work in cast aggregate, which was sold in their shop. Because Alexander no longer had his original, he used the MoMA gift shop replica as his model in order to fill requests from Perls, Gerald Cramer, and Eric Estorick for bronze casts of his most recognized work. In effect, the work they bought was a variant from a replica. Ironically, one of these casts was sold to the Tate Gallery through Estorick's Grosvenor Gallery. It is not clear how the sale went—whether Perls had sold it first to Cramer, in tandem with Estorick, or whether all three sold it to the Tate. Since the bronze edition traced back to the artist, additional due diligence might not have seemed necessary.

Unavoidable also was confusion over cast numbers, a relatively new practice more associated with marketing than authenticating. Of the few signature Archipenko pieces which were easy to sell for Perls, the earlier ones didn't always have numbers—and if they did, there was no consistency. Rather than cast numbers, which became a tangle of contradictions, Perls described the inscriptions as "runes," a coded inscription that identified the work. In her thorough study of Archipenko's issues with variants, Katherine Michaelsen also reviewed the problem of cast numbers:

> When Perls took on Archipenko in 1957 he encouraged him to cast properly-numbered bronze editions of his sculptures. However, regarding the dating, Perls has expressed his opinion that the dealer's only task is to promote and sell the work, that dating and everything else concerning the creation of the work are entirely the responsibility of the artist himself.[5]

Questionable casts, unauthorized works, and irregular or redundant cast numbers didn't faze Perls. He considered himself the authority, and his collectors would just have to trust him. It was his game and his rules.

Confusion was also blossoming in Alexander's correspondence related to shipping, prices, and redundant cast numbers. Like Perls, Alexander didn't have the habit of recording numbers accurately, which was to directly taint his relationship with some of his dealers abroad. Not always consistent, Alexander, on occasion, forgetfully changed the fractional or repeated a number. For example, there are an unlimited number of authorized casts, usually made to order, of *Flat Torso* (fig. 17) from 1914/15. The latest casts of *Flat Torso*, which were done under the supervision of Archipenko in the United States, are numbered but do not have a fractional which would indicate a designated numerical limit.

While letters of authenticity may have satisfied the customer, over the years they've also lost their significance, even if they were accompanied by a photograph of the actual work. In some instances these images might be of another cast from the edition, or of a work that was restored years later.

Much of the activity initiated between dealers, dealer-collectors, collectors, and donors to public collections during this period raised questions. All of this unevenness of documentation created a tangle of doubt that infected the auction houses as well. This was a time when auction houses catalogued without adequate research, often doing the equivalent of cutting and pasting the same provenance on more than one bronze cast of an edition. It is only in recent years that the major auction houses have begun insisting upon expertise before consignment—and understanding what this entails for works by

Fig. 52 Alexander Archipenko (1887–1964), © ARS, NY. *Woman Combing Her Hair*, 1915, bronze, $13^3/_4$ x $3^1/_4$ x $3^1/_8$ in. (35 x 8.3 x 8 cm) including base. Acquired through the Lillie P. Bliss request. The Museum of Modern Art, New York, NY, U.S.A. Digital image © The Museum of Modern Art/Licensed by SCALA/Art Resource, NY.

Archipenko. It wouldn't be until the following year, however, that Alexander confronted the extent to which he was vulnerable to the greed of all the second parties involved in the process of bringing his art to the marketplace.

As 1959 came to a close and winter gave way to spring, Alexander and I developed a satisfying daily rhythm. Working long hours in our New York studios and meeting at his apartment at night, our life together continued to grow and shift. I was no longer just the mentee, fellow artist, and lover of Alexander. I had become his domestic partner and confidante.

When he encouraged me to join him in Europe the summer of 1960, I felt cherished. He missed me and wanted me with him. However, as I anticipated joining him in Paris, marriage was the last thought on my mind.

Chapter Ten
Married to Archipenko

After our initial meeting in the lobby of my Paris hotel and lunch at a café, Alexander asked me to help him with some correspondence. Although we were very happy to be seeing each other, it was evident that he didn't have the preoccupations of a tourist. He was there to consolidate his European plans and juggle the many players involved.

At the end of that July in 1960, a touring retrospective of sixty-eight sculptures from 1909 to 1959 would be opening in Saarbrücken, Germany. Alexander's goal was to extend the tour of these works beyond Germany—perhaps to Switzerland and, hopefully, London—to avoid the high cost of transporting the exhibit back to the States. He'd scheduled a return trip to London to meet with David Thomas of the Arts Council of Great Britain, to discuss the possibility of exhibiting at the Tate Gallery. If he could schedule the full show intact, have the shipping costs covered, and sell enough works, the financial goals of the project would be met.

As he dictated, I drafted letters in English that were translated and typed into French by a hotel secretary available for that purpose. Divvying the works up into more than one simultaneous exhibition was a complicated maneuver which Alexander was prepared to attempt. Because he had enough work to spill over, he thought he could place his work in two galleries at the same time. These efforts sometimes came to cross-purposes, especially when Archipenko approached contacts from the same city. He didn't account for the fact that museums and galleries are not only in competition with each other, but also cooperate with one another. For example, in Zurich he first contacted Dr. R. Wehrli, the director of the Kunsthaus museum, hoping for a show. When they let him know they weren't interested, he then contacted Dr. Willy Rotzler, curator at the Kunstgewerbe-museum, who also had to refuse him because both institutions were under the same governing body. Alexander had no idea why there should be any conflict or embarrassment. He didn't always understand the underpinnings of the network he needed to sustain his position.

Although the friends he had left in Paris, which included Sonia Delaunay and Joseph Csáky as well as Severini and Survage, had introduced him to anyone they thought might be useful, Paris was difficult. There was an invisible resistance to his work, with no official and only tentative commercial interest in an exhibition. He was an outsider there. While the other European countries had a more international approach, the French government preferred to support artists who lived and worked in France, perpetuating Paris as the art capital of the world. Perhaps if Alexander had remained in Paris, it would have been different.

Although his reputation was based on the past and no dealer truly championed his recent work, Alexander still included his entire lifetime output in the wave of retrospective solo exhibitions he was attempting arrange. His choice of works for the Saarbrücken show was, in a way, a physical version of the monograph *Fifty Creative Years*. It was always self-evident to Alexander that the best way to show his overall contribution to the visual arts was to present his work as a group, arranged both in chronological order and by specific themes and mediums. This was the very same reasoning which guided curatorial practice in museums and private galleries when an individual artist was presented. Alexander's most current works, he believed, were more accessible when shown with his previous output, thus establishing a link. Now I would be by his side as he renewed his international credibility with an ongoing retrospective.

Except for their normal anxiety about my welfare, my parents had no objection to my being a professional artist living and exhibiting in Europe. Using the money left to me by my paternal grandfather when he died, I'd booked a ticket to Paris and reserved a room at a high-quality tourist hotel near the Louvre. That I was going to Paris specifically to join Alexander wouldn't occur to my family. Because I was one of Archipenko's favorite ex-students and a young colleague, they would have assumed that if Alexander happened to be in Paris, he'd be as helpful as he'd been in New York. To my parents, our actual intimacy and the fact that we were inseparable was invisible.

In letters back home, I maintained the deception. On June 3, 1960, I wrote to my parents on Le Grand Hotel Du Louvre stationery:

Dear Mother and Dad,

All is well. Everyone I have met has been extremely gracious. Yesterday I had lunch with Mr. and Mrs. Survage, in his studio. He is a very old and good friend of Archipenko. The day before I had seen his paintings in the Museum of Modern Art. It was extremely interesting. The day before a French painter I had met in New York took me to a number of studios of young artists, all quite well know [sic] but not particularly impressive. You would be shocked by their living conditions. – My studio on 8th Ave. is a Palace in comparison. – However, they all own automobiles, and have exhibited and visited New York. The studios I visited surround Brancusi's larger one. They are very old cement shacks with skylights. The best artist of entire group was a young American sculptor – who was not that great – but at least sincere and technically capable – also young enough to mature. Tamir, the French painter wanted me to rent one of the studios for $70.00 a month – but I am not particularly interested. – I rather have the fresh air of Switzerland. – also, the privacy.

Twice I was insulted in French at a Café – for being a foreigner but was also defended in French. Quite a scene. – It was probably done for the amusement of the tourists and seemed very put on – theatrical.

This morning I will visit the Louvre again, which is only one block away.

Write to me in care of this hotel. If I move they can always forward it.

All my love, Frances[1]

Although we never made the trip, I failed to mention that I was planning to go to Switzerland with Archipenko. It's no accident that I was also vague about Alexander's attendance at lunch with Léopold and Germaine Survage, Alexander's oldest friends in Paris. My chatty letters gave no reason to suspect that Alexander was the reason I was in France, or that I was spending my days and nights with him. Explaining to my parents that I wanted cheaper quarters, I eventually checked out of my expensive hotel on the Right Bank and moved to the Hotel Trianon on the Left, where I joined Alexander in his modest rooms.

Of course, in Paris, it was no secret that we were together. As Alexander introduced me to Gino Severini and Léopold Survage, his old cohorts were happy for him. Picasso had a much younger wife, as did Pablo Casals. It simply suggested that Alexander was still vigorous. There was no sin in that.

However, something else was slowly developing in the summer of 1960. For reasons of propriety and social comfort, the Survages encouraged us to marry before we traveled together. Appearances and practicalities were important to Germaine. Wisely protective of me—I had obviously passed her scrutiny—she was sure I'd be more "comfortable" if married.

The 1960s was still a world of couples. Even though I was included in invitations as a courtesy to Alexander, I was self-conscious and uncomfortable if called upon to introduce myself before we were married. It was his career, not mine, which had the capital. Until we were married, I was often perceived as a tagalong student, a "plus one." Marriage would change that, and Germaine knew it. The Survages were even more concerned about Alexander's potential loneliness and the ultimate protection of his work, since he no longer had any family. Together since 1918 and childless, Léopold and

Germaine depended upon each other's companionship and imagined Alexander's isolation in America.

Although I was initially hesitant to marry, I supposed it was inevitable. We'd been together for five years and, in a sense, "engaged" for some time—that is to say, we seemed unable to part. We were bonded. It was clear that he truly cared for me, and whatever my attachment to him was—perhaps this was impossible to determine, as it remained unspoken—from our first summer together I was hooked, or, as my brother wrote, I loved Alexander "irrationally."

Even as an adolescent, I was at odds with what was normally wished for by girls and their parents. Finding a husband was not my goal, and as I explained to my friends at a slumber party, the only way I would consider marriage was "many times," as the thought of living with the same man for an entire lifetime struck me as very boring. Also, having children and living the way the people around me lived was not something I found compelling. I wanted to "grow up," but it had to be by my own definition, not an imitation of a model which I found mundane.

Not only was my marriage to Alexander not ordinary, it was strangely surreal. He never proposed. He just told me the date. I'm sure we talked about it, as it related to our travel plans, but I don't remember a specific conversation. It was not the memorable experience those events are fabled to be.

Germaine took it upon herself to help Alexander fill out the forms in order to post the banns which were required ten days before the civil ceremony, which was scheduled for August 1, 1960. Our plan was to enjoy Paris during the waiting period and then travel to Saarbrücken for the opening of Alexander's sculpture exhibition once we were married. While we waited, we visited Alexander's old friends, especially the Survages and Gino Severini, who still maintained his studio in Paris. I remember Severini as jolly, showing us how, when he painted, he always wore a paper hat made of that day's newspaper. These studio visits were particularly poignant for Alexander. Alexander's last studio in Paris— which Giacometti had rented much later—was once again vacant in the artists' cul de sac. Tinguely had set up a talking refrigerator outside in the shared courtyard, and after we were introduced, he offered, "Have a Coca-Cola." When I opened the refrigerator's door, it started swearing at me in French.

Publishing banns also required that we inform my parents about the pending marriage. I began to watch for return mail.

The 15th arrondissement town hall that doubled as a police precinct had the stale air of Gauloise cigarettes and windows that were never opened. An official performed the formal civil ceremony one time and then mumbled something in French as each couple passed individually in front of him. When it was our turn, we replied "oui" and were legally bound. Since the official spoke as quickly as possible, and in French, I made believe that I understood what I was saying "oui" to.

Of course you are never quite sure what you're saying "yes" to in a marriage, but as I said "oui," I made a silent wish that I would not be blind to whatever it was that I needed to know and do, and that I'd have the stamina to accomplish it.

In retrospect, that moment in time, our marriage in Paris, appears as a starting point. The future is always unknown, but my marriage gave me an invisible map that would always automatically guide me back to Alexander—his work and his life. Early on, I'd known in my heart that he wanted me to be like him—or even better, wanted to make his interests mine—in a kind of creative perpetuity.

After the ceremony we went to lunch with the Survages at La Closerie des Lilas, a restaurant with a place in art history, famous as a Surrealist hangout in the early twentieth century. Alexander and Léopold were nostalgic, and there was a warmth of feeling between us as if we'd all successfully completed a project. Unfortunately, this was not my family's reaction.

Surprised to receive a letter from my brother the day after the ceremony, I opened the envelope hoping he was wishing me good luck. Instead, Steve expressed utter repulsion in a letter ugly with rage: "How could you do this to our parents and our family? You're a pervert and sexual deviant." There was no letter from my parents who, my brother claimed, "were shocked."

I had broken the rules.

What were the rules? If anything, Alexander and I believed that rules were made to be broken. We were cohorts. This was our creative alliance. It was not just a desire for fun that prompted the dictum that rules were best broken. Rules were best broken when vitality was at stake. The risk of breaking the majority's rules was isolation, for in so doing you separated yourself from the crowd, or at least the coherent social group. Creative artists were always doing this. It was how they defined themselves and their work. When Alexander and I married, we had a civil ceremony, thus obeying the rules, and at the same time broke the social propriety of age grouping (the mating rules of the game). My family saw our action as "unnatural" and a social embarrassment.

I knew what I had to do. I tore the letter into the smallest pieces possible and then flushed them down the very noisy, highly pressurized toilet that was part of our modest hotel suite at the Hotel Trianon on the Avenue du Maine. I never told Alexander. Then I wrote two letters. To my parents:

Dear Mother and Dad,

I received a letter from Steve today and I am now terribly concerned about you and Dad. Please try to be reasonable and understand that it was not such a horrible thing that I did. – I only deceived you, because there was no sense in telling you, I never expected you to understand and I never will. Steve wrote me that he could never understand why and that it was probably because my reasons were so "strange" and "unnatural". My reasons are complicated, but they are not so – out of this world. It is a very natural thing for us to be married, although it may seem quite odd and disturbing in Scarsdale. Dad is probably more ashamed and embarrassed than anything else. I understand it is a very frustrating situation for both of you. Please try to think positively or everything will seem much worse than it really is for you. And know that I intend to be happy with my husband, since I will not be happy without him.

Tomorrow morning we are going to Saarbrucken. The exhibit there is opening earlier than we expected. Probably we will go to Nice afterwards, for business reasons—So, we cancelled our reservations in Normandy.

I am very anxious to see both of you and try to make things a little easier for you. Unless, it would be easier for you not to see me.

My love to you both,

Frances

To my brother I wrote:

Dear Steve,

I really regret that you can not understand even a little, but then of course, I live for completely different reasons than you do. Perhaps someday you will be able to accept life beyond the suburbs of Westchester, but I rather doubt it. Please don't apply your normal and "natural" standards to me. Life for me is much more complicated and richer than that. And, my "motives" do not pertain at all to your standards. I love my parents, but I do not and can not become their image of me. And my "deception" was I thought really for their benefit, certainly not for mine. Since, either way I will get their anathema, and either way I will not change. And I have accepted the fact that my "basic character" has many contradictions, and perhaps now you will have to also. So, if you use your imagination a little without the fear of being illogical perhaps you will begin to understand, and not be too righteous.

I love my husband very irrationally and really prefer it that way. We don't count years, money or possessions. As much as possible we are free. And, I have no intention of wasting my life by feeling guilty for what I have done to my parents. They will recover as soon as they want to. I suppose this ends any further discussion about my marriage, which to my mind is not any kind of dramatic tragedy or unnatural act.

If my letter is too strong please do not be hurt by it, since I always think of you with love and affection,

Frances

Now married, with the letters to my family on their way, we left in time for the opening in Saarbrücken.

* * *

I saw her inching her way through the crowd in my direction, smiling broadly, wearing a tailored herringbone suit with beefed up shoulder pads, carefully groomed but with a bad haircut. Because I spoke no German, I immediately repelled most curiosity seekers. Speaking in impeccable English with undertones of a German accent, the woman introduced herself as a journalist from Alexandria, Egypt.

From her questions, it was clear that the interview was to be about me rather than the show. Our commitment had gone public and she wanted a story about Archipenko's new wife. My policy when accompanying Alexander for his work was not to talk about myself. It was about him and his work. With this show, Archipenko was boosting his European career. That was the news. In my thinking, our marriage should be of interest only to us. As I look back, I realize that my role to some extent was "arm candy," a vantage point I found amusing. However, having become an object of curiosity that tickled people's imagination, I was uncomfortable. Wearing the felt hat Alexander had given me usually made me feel as I wished to—disguised.

Now I was face-to-face with the reporter from Egypt. Aggressive and self-assured, her clipped British accent almost covered her German undercarriage. "May I ask, what is your background?"

The reporter and I stared at each other. This felt like an affront, not a question. Although Archipenko's work in museums and Jewish private collections had been labeled "degenerate" and confiscated by the Nazis, he was now being honored and reintroduced in Germany as some of these very same museums reacquired his works. National and ethnic identity were sensitive topics that continued to surface well after World War II, however, and certain people were still interested in Archipenko's background—and mine as well. Returning the reporter's smile, I gave her my answer: "American Jewish."

I suppose shocking people can be amusing in a pointless sort of way. But I realized too late that this particular mutual faux pas was like slapstick comedy. Still smiling, I continued, "And what are you doing in Egypt, and could you tell me the political position of your newspaper?" Turning around, she walked away as decisively as she had approached. I didn't tell Alexander about the incident. I enjoyed seeing this bold woman flee the room. But my own boldness was rare. I remained low-key even though, as the artist's wife, I would soon find myself thrust into a cosmopolitan mélange moving from country to country where I was often interviewed and photographed.

Meanwhile, the party was in his honor, and Alexander was having a good time, unconcerned about the response to his retrospective. His later works—including some sculpto-paintings—had a lukewarm reception from the local German art journalists. Multi-material constructions from the 1950s including *Cleopatra* (fig. 30)—who had regained her original name—and *Orange and Black* (fig. 31) were regarded as they were in New York: as oddities. The eclecticism in Alexander's practice was not understood in a positive way since it was not perceived as sequential, but uncomfortably chaotic. As usual, it was his signature early work that attracted the attention.

My thoughts drifted to the reception which would be waiting for us back in New York. On August 7, I wrote from Germany.

Dear Mother and Dad,

I have been in Saarbrucken since Wednesday but have not had a moment free. We are living in a magnificent modernized palace on the top of a small mountain as guests of the State. It is being used as a radio and television station. We have been interviewed on the radio and they have filmed a television program of the exhibit. Tomorrow they are making a separate program on film of me and my work, sort of "person to person." We have been wined and dined by the mayor and all the various ministers of culture – and are always being chauffeured around. And we have been invited to come back and work in a very beautiful studio, whenever we can and for long as we want to. It is really an unbelievable paradise here. The museum has bought two bronzes and all five drawings and would like to order a commission if they can get the funds. – Germany is really an amazing place. – In Saarbrucken 70% of the city was destroyed and the population extremely depleted and now they have skyscrapers and museums and lots of little blond babies.

Probably next week we will go to Muenster. My address here is: . . . They will be very happy to forward any mail. I am very anxious to hear from you.

All my love,

Frances

They never responded.

When we arrived at the home of Hanna Bekker vom Rath on the outskirts of Frankfurt, I sat staring at her, unable to speak, not knowing how to respond to my first patroness. Alexander had arranged the meeting, just as he was arranging other aspects of my career. He generously promoted my art whenever he had the opportunity, but the acceptance and showing of my work simply because I was a protégé of Archipenko felt so awkward that I was left speechless.

A heavyset older woman, Frau Bekker vom Roth said she recalled me from a brief visit to Woodstock, although I didn't remember it. I found her overly friendly in a grandmotherly way, which only added to my discomfort. I was struck by her untamed garden that surrounded an overgrown quince tree ripe with fruit.

Even though she was about to exhibit my sculptures, I had nothing to say to this famous art dealer who had established the Frankfurter Kunstkabinett as one of the first new galleries after World War II. She nurtured German artists and intellectuals throughout her life, and saved many German Expressionist paintings from being confiscated during the Nazi regime. In 1949, she had exhibited fourteen of Archipenko's most recent drawings.

With Delacorte I had been so withdrawn that I couldn't even remember his first name, and now I was having the same disconnect with Frau Bekker vom Rath. As she took us through her painting studio and showed us around her art collection, she described her enthusiasm for my work. I had no answer, feeling trapped and anxious to leave.

As the ways of the art world now became my concern, all that was patronage and packaging irritated me. Negotiations went on behind closed doors, with words used to describe art objects that were better applied to a shipment of potatoes; an artist and his work could be eventually corrupted under financial pressure and, counterintuitively, this would universally signal an enviable success. The critics who wandered through exhibitions were always under multiple pressures to instruct their public and to please their publisher's advertisers. So many interconnections could keep a spider busy working overtime. All of these thoughts of how little I knew about what was under the surface just made my head spin. And I imagined there was much more I didn't want to know.

Alexander took all this in his stride. Even if I wasn't adept at self-promotion, meeting with gallery owners was all part of Alexander's focus for both of us. He also arranged for my show to travel on in the fall from Germany to the Drian Gallery in London. He knew how to compartmentalize, and he played the game like a professional. I didn't. That is not to say that Alexander couldn't unravel when he felt betrayed—but his profound loyalty in friendship endured well beyond self-interest.

In Paris we'd been approached at La Coupole by a sculptor who'd recently seen some of Archipenko's early works on exhibition at the Picasso Museum in Antibes. From his description, it was clear the plasters were those which had been stored for Alexander since his departure from the south of France after World War I by his friends the Verdiers.

The final stop on our itinerary was a spontaneous trip to Nice.

* * *

The modest café was on a narrow street in walking distance from our hotel on the Promenade des Anglais. The setting was out of Babar the Elephant King. Jean and Zena Verdier were sitting at a table with a third person, Zena's sister, whose skin was a remarkable shade of blue. On this extremely bright day, they sat protected from the heat of the sun at the side street venue.

Exuding a fair amount of emotion, Zena and Jean greeted Alexander and then made introductions all around. In Paris, Zena had actually lived with Alexander before leaving him for Jean, but they'd all remained close friends. After a delicious light lunch of salade Niçoise and a bottle of rosé, the reunion proceeded to some strong demi-cafés. Once we'd parted ways with the sister, Jean hailed a taxi, and the four of us were off to the next part of our adventure.

The Verdiers led us through property overgrown with weeds to a small building that had been used for long-term storage. It was moldy and in disarray, as if it had already been rummaged through. They had lived on this property before they left France. Before 1923, Alexander had arranged with the Verdiers to store his work when he left, at that time not knowing that he would ultimately stay in the United States for the remainder of his life. They, in turn, later left Nice. After decades abroad because of World War II, much of the time spent in South America, Zena and her husband had just returned. Old and poor, most of their money gone, they lived with Zena's blue sister. Her skin condition was called argyria, a result of taking colloidal silver for some minor ailment.

The Verdiers' antique furniture, also damply stored, was worm-eaten and worthless. Their only remaining financial resource was Alexander's sculptures, some of which were in disintegrating cardboard cartons packed with newspapers from the 1920s. They pleaded that all they had left to subsist on was the Archipenko art they could sell and the hospitality of Zena's sister.

For Alexander, these plasters were a symbol of his years in Paris and his early fame. They were also what his current collectors wanted in bronze. Zena knew this, and it turned out that dealers and collectors had been contacting them after the exhibition in Antibes. Although they had only been with Zena for safekeeping and by rights Alexander owned them, he generously offered to buy back his old plaster models. Gently negotiating with his old friends, he retrieved what he could.

Because Alexander no longer remembered what he had left in the Verdiers' care, he had only a vague sense of how many pieces should be there. He didn't retrieve all that was his—and he accepted this with grace. Soon after his death, I would discover that several works with a Verdier provenance had found their way to the Hirshhorn collection.

As Alexander and I headed for Le Havre to board the ocean liner back to New York, he was grateful that his rather cavalier treatment of all the work he'd left behind over the years would be a mixed blessing. Even though some had slipped out of his hands, he appreciated that he could retrieve so much which had an unquestionable early provenance.

As we neared port in New York City, I was facing a more personal dilemma. We'd be moving into Alexander's apartment as a married couple, and I had yet to receive a letter from my parents. I decided to avoid contacting them rather than cause more discomfort. They were no doubt trying to figure out how and if they would present Alexander to their circle of friends as their son-in-law—especially at the country club.

Once again, Alexander was my mentor, but this time he was teaching me how to be skillful in life and emotionally generous with my parents. He urged me to meet with them before we returned to Europe for the winter: "They're right to be upset, and they'll still be your parents long after I am no longer here. Don't dismiss their feelings."

* * *

The train from Grand Central Station left me in Scarsdale, and I doggedly took the long stroll up Garth Road to my parents' apartment. Anticipating the smell of chicken soup, I got off the elevator on the fifth floor. As I rang the doorbell I could hear the animated conversation of my nephews, Jeffrey and Lowell, on the other side of the door, their footsteps muted by the thick wall-to-wall carpeting. I was ready for a full family dinner. Jeffrey opened the door. Lowell was still small enough to pick up and hug after dropping my bag of presents.

My parents remained seated opposite my brother and his wife in the formal living room on the two occasional chairs and the tufted sofa. An untouched iridescent dish of cashews rested on the glass oval table between them.

The only one to unglue was my mother. She rose from her shell. "What would everyone like to drink before dinner?"

We all assumed that the time for greetings had passed, and I swiftly made my way to the bathroom to tidy up from the long walk from the station.

After handing out a small, carefully wrapped present to everyone, I knelt on the floor and played with my nephews and their new toys before dinner.

It was much easier than I'd imagined. Taking Alexander's suggestion, I imitated my parents, acting as if the marriage had never happened. Since there was nothing they could do to change the reality, their strategy was to say nothing, to stay emotionally uncommitted and not make a scene. Out of sight, out of mind. Perhaps they thought Alexander and I would settle down in Europe, they would have an exciting place to visit, and they'd never have to worry about explaining Alexander to their friends. Whatever they were thinking, they behaved toward me in a calm and low-key way, without threats or demands. Nixon and Kennedy were the dinner conversation, as well as "the changing times." All that was unspoken remained so. The only thing that was different was the narrow gold wedding band on my finger.

Even though it would be almost another year before they would face Alexander, they did eventually acknowledge that I was married, giving me a wedding gift: a good set of white China. Unexpectedly, however, during this period, Alexander and I enjoyed my paternal grandmother's acceptance of my choice. My grandfather had always encouraged my independence from my parents, and after he died, my grandmother carried on her own minor rebellion against my father, her only child.

Insisting upon having Alexander and me to dinner at least once a week at the West Village studio apartment she'd moved to after she was widowed, she always produced huge amounts of delicious food so that Alexander would eat well. After these visits, I wouldn't have to shop or cook for the remainder of the week. She frequently expressed her rejection of my parent's rejection of my marriage, enthusing, "I love Alexander too because I see he makes you happy. He is a good man." When we were with her, I was always reminded of my grandfather's generous support and confidence in my career as an artist, and of his intuitive respect for Archipenko the first time he met him. Meanwhile, as we settled into Alexander's apartment, the transition to married couple felt seamless.

Alexander enjoyed a form of cooking which was informal and thrifty. It was the first time I saw leftover pasta being consciously recycled for the next day's meal. If we ate at home alone, Alexander and I would often cook together or at least share the cleanup. Then it would seem an occasion, not a chore, remarkably different from the domesticity which I knew and expected growing up. As a child I was never around when anything was actually cleaned or cooked. The door to the kitchen was closed before and after dinner; the evening meal just appeared on the table. Things were made magically—from beds to cookies.

Now I became interested in watching my peers, such as my brother's wife or a young married friend, who were cooks and homemakers. I used candles and cloth napkins, even if they didn't match. I put mustard in the salad dressing and learned to make crème caramel, Alexander's favorite dessert. Whenever possible, I made something with cinnamon for dessert, to get rid of the smells of meat and garlic in the apartment. When we had company, I tried to imitate my mother, who could put together a meal for invited guests, take off her charming hostess apron, and sit down as if she'd just arrived.

Alexander, I believe, was disappointed by my growing domesticity. For him, my main roles were up-and-coming professional artist, ex-student, wife, and companion. He was particularly adamant on one point. "Don't waste your time cleaning the apartment. Go do your work; I have someone who cleans." Here, Alexander was "old school." Domestic chores were for domestics. It sounds a bit "upstairs/downstairs," and especially when you consider that we were living in a very run-down apartment building in a run-down neighborhood with nothing to spare, it was a little peculiar—just as fantastic as his still hearing his dead wife Angelica ring him on a bell in the middle of the night. These ideas were all shades of his past which waved him toward another way of managing daily life.

Although marriage seemed to mark no new stage in our relationship, it was clear that Alexander liked introducing me as his wife. He wrote to an old friend, "While in Europe I married an ex-student of mine and solitude doesn't disturb me anymore."[2] In a letter written two months after our wedding, Alexander explained to our insurance agent, "Yesterday, September 25, 1960 my car was driven by my wife, Mrs. Frances Gray Archipenko, in South Nyack and due to an abrupt stop she hit another car."[3] He also may have begun feeling more responsible for me. He had always cautioned me to "watch" myself "on the street" when I went out. But now, as we walked together in New York City, I felt like a child when he told me to "look both ways" at the curb.

In contrast, I was being increasingly cast in the role of future protector of Alexander's legacy. And his work needed protection.

Chapter Eleven
Risks

Eric Estorick escorted us down a flight of stairs to the cramped subterranean storage room of the Grosvenor Gallery. The ambiance was "bomb shelter." With its few chairs and a desk, it had the feeling of a hideaway, not at all the kind of place you'd expect an international art dealer to be receiving an internationally acclaimed artist.

Although we needed to be in New York for most of 1961 as Alexander worked twelve-hour days preparing shows for the coming year, he decided that we should make a short trip to London in May just before the opening of Eric Estorick's Archipenko show at the Grosvenor. Estorick was mounting the exhibit independently of Alexander, who owned only one work in the show (because Estorick had yet to pay him for it). The other pieces in the exhibit were owned by collectors or had been acquired by Estorick on the secondary market for resale.

Wearing his signature black, in this case a black cashmere turtleneck sweater which seemed too warm for the sunny day in London, Estorick settled behind the desk and glanced uneasily at me. His citrus-scented cologne permeated the room. All I knew was that we had been invited here to look at a sculpture. Now that I was Archipenko's wife, my presence as a witness added a degree of strength to his position. It implied that even after Archipenko's inevitable death, there would be someone around who was young and who might champion his work. I would be the person to eventually follow up on all contracts. I was the unknown quantity—the X factor—the artist's wife and future heir.

When Estorick produced and placed on the desk a bronze cast of Archipenko's *Flat Torso*—which had been consigned to him by "a private person"—Alexander pushed back his chair and bellowed, "Whoever cast this work is a criminal and a forger."

Also jumping up from his chair, Estorick shouted back at Alexander. "I'll call my lawyer immediately and start a libel suit against you. How dare you accuse me of casting this sculpture? What's more, I won't tell you where I got it."

When we left the Grosvenor Gallery with all bridges burned, Alexander had no idea that his arrangement with Estorick would materialize into serious questions about authenticity and risk factors for collectors, even in his own lifetime. It was time for a social call. After the confrontation with Estorick, Alexander set up our first meeting with the Goeritz family.

* * *

Mrs. Goeritz's apartment was soft and light-filled, in contrast to the somber darkness and angry confrontation that had recently occurred in the Grosvenor basement.

It was Erich Goeritz's oldest son, Andrew, who had loaned Eric Estorick the controversial *Statuette* (fig. 50), and whom Alexander had alerted about the unauthorized casting two years earlier. Andrew was in charge of the family art collection, which included a huge cache of Archipenko works from before World War I. Andrew saw Estorick as a valued friend and confidant, but their connection felt odd and potentially confusing, not only in the Goeritz legacy but also in the authenticity of Archipenko's bronze editions. We were there to mend fences.

Mrs. Erich Goeritz, although not well enough to leave her bedroom, was very animated when she greeted Alexander, thrilled to be receiving such an important artist. As she reclined in an elegant bed encased in crisp and exquisitely embroidered sheets, Mrs. Goeritz and Alexander traveled through time to the Berlin of their past. On the wall across from the bed was a sun-dappled reclining nude portrait of her with her two young sons by Lovis Corinth.

In the adjacent living room, Andrew's beautiful British wife—probably just about my age—was watching their two small sons, who were all cleaned up to be their grandmother's next visitors. The setting was impressionistic, with the light in the apartment, the translucent skin of its inhabitants, and the naked children in the painting, one of whom was Andrew Goeritz, the father of the two actual little boys playing games in the next room.

Twenty-five years later, one of those little boys, now the same age his father had been when I met him in London in 1961, greeted me in Washington as a representative of the Goeritz family at the opening of the 1986 exhibition *Alexander Archipenko: A Centennial Tribute*, a tour of the works which his family had saved in the Tel Aviv Museum.

Remarkably, neither the Goeritz's holdings of Archipenko's works nor the problem of unauthorized casts was brought up in conversation that day. This meeting served a social purpose. It honored something generational, something which only Mrs. Goeritz and Alexander fully shared.

With Estorick no longer representing him—even though Estorick continued dealing with his work in the secondary market—it was inevitable that Alexander would seek other dealers to represent him in London and abroad. He immediately began using our time in London to seek other possibilities. While simultaneously presenting similar proposals to the Leicester Gallery and Hanover Gallery, Alexander also met with Stephanie Maison of the Matthiesen Gallery. He was taking no chances that he'd miss out on an exhibition in London.

In a letter to Mrs. Maison, who ultimately agreed to a show, Alexander enumerated suggestions for a formal contract in which her gallery would have exclusivity in Great Britain and the right to sell in other countries. At the end of the list of ten suggestions for an agreement he added:

> As I have already told you, Mr. Estorick, unfortunately, has bought a number of my works from the Perls Gallery, my New York Gallery, and Mr. Estorick plans to have an exhibition in the summer. I do hope that this will not affect our collaboration, especially because I decidedly wish to avoid all and any cooperation with Mr. Estorick under all circumstances.
>
> I shall greatly appreciate your early reply. If, as I hope it will be, it is favorable, I shall immediately order new bronze casts for my important exhibition at your Gallery.[1]

My retelling of our London experience of failure, frustration, and ultimate success is distorted by time. I was still in my twenties when all of this occurred, and my interpretation was flavored by my own inexperience. Alexander could not be wrong!

Always giving Alexander the benefit of the doubt and the most positive spin, I saw him as brave, noble, and beyond criticism; he was transmitting a metaphysical message in the form of visual art. I told myself that he was ambitious for his work's survival because he believed in its importance. Being multifaceted, Alexander was not without his material needs, so he tolerated conventional materialistic thinking as part of the general mix. However, he was profoundly propelled by deeper concerns. He believed everyone was born a genius, although this birthright might be reduced by life's hard knocks. How he defined genius went back to Bergson. All of these thoughts could send me adrift. I do know he never projected failure. There was always something else around the bend—another country, city, museum, art dealer, collector, or lecture to be given.

When Alexander had suggested to Erica Brausen of the Hanover Gallery—who'd alerted him to Estorick's unofficial castings—that she exhibit his work, she eventually backed away from her initial interest. Very particular about works having cast numbers, she also wanted letters of authentication from the artist indicating limited editions. By this point in time, Alexander had started the habit of inscribing little codes ("runes," as Perls called them) as well as cast numbers—which by now he had lost track of, resulting in the occasional redundancy—and indicating the inscription on the letters of authenticity. However, the taint of a scandal was already touching Alexander. The word was out, probably through Gerald Cramer—Archipenko's agent in Switzerland—that there was some inconsistency in cast numbers and that, in certain instances, cast numbers were not even inscribed.

As we left London to return to New York, Alexander remained unconcerned about the growing controversies about his work. He was happy, believing he had found a new dealer and expecting to have a London exhibit. He certainly had no premonition of the extent to which the maelstrom over unauthorized casts and cast numbering would grow. He was thinking of other things. When we returned to New York in June 1961, Alexander was continuing to arrange my life for me. This time, however, it wasn't a new exhibit that he surprised me with.

* * *

We could have been going on an excursion to a museum or to Canal Street as we left the apartment one morning together, Alexander casually remarking that he had something to show me.

The sun was hitting the pavement in front of the house on Bedford Street in the West Village when we arrived and started our way down the three gray painted concrete steps that led to a hidden front doorway. Alexander rang the bell and immediately a comfortable older woman with gray hair and a clean but slightly dowdy dress greeted us. Her husband was a shadow in the background. The hallway we entered was dim and occupied by a staircase that wound up three stories, taking up at least thirty percent of the internal space of the building. Next to the below ground-floor entranceway was the equivalent of a basement front parlor where one could see people's legs as they passed by in the street. This led to a kitchen with an old brick fireplace and a window which looked out onto a landscaped garden in the backyard.

Because it was old and had never been extensively renovated, the house did not smell fresh, even though it was relatively clean. The subbasement smelled of New York drainage, and all the windows, along with their sills, accumulated unending traffic dust. However, the garden had a peach tree, relatively fresh air, and daily sun. Since the house was very narrow, consisting of one awkward duplex and two small separate apartments, it never had the look of a conventional home with a real bedroom, dining room, and living room. As he showed me around, Alexander had an air of ownership. It was clear. Without consulting me, Alexander had already bought the building.

Fig. 53 Alexander Archipenko, *Kimono*, 1961, bronze, 31½ in. (80 cm), private collection

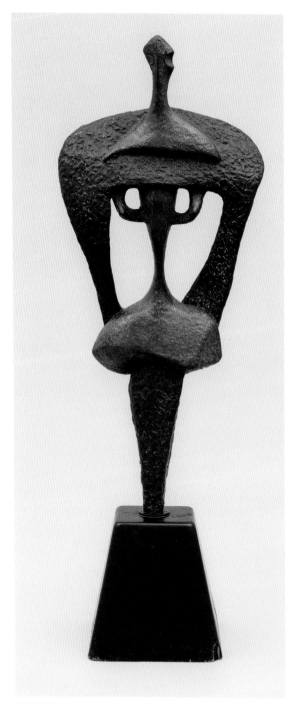

Fig. 54 Alexander Archipenko, *Tapering Figure*, 1961, bronze, 29 1/2 x 13 x 4 in.
(74.9 x 33 x 10.2 cm), Frances Gray Collection

Fig. 55 Alexander Archipenko, *Linear Oriental*, 1961, plaster, 24³/₄ x 13⁷/₈ x 11³/₄ in. (63 x 35.3 x 30 cm), Saarland Museum, Saarbrücken, Germany

With his growing wealth from the new interest in his work, Alexander wanted to own his own space. Determined that we move from the apartment on 19th Street which he'd shared for so many years with Angelica, he wanted a fresh start and a permanent home that would lift his spirit and reflect his success. The other apartments that we looked at together didn't interest him. This was a serious upgrade, a town house with a yard for Sappho. For the short time we were together, this house became ours.

My part in this new life had been important in his choice. As Alexander was also determined that I would be successful as an artist, I had my own studio on the fourth floor, where I could continue working toward exhibitions. All of this was a surprise, but I had a sense of déjà vu. My future unrolled in front of me with a certain amount of odd predictability. He had arranged where I'd exhibit, and now he arranged where I'd live.

We slowly settled in to our house on Bedford Street. Married, working, and running a household, we established a comfortable routine. Early in the morning, I headed for my studio on the fourth floor, and Alexander left for a full day of work at his studio.

When he wasn't able to network in person, Alexander conducted business from his loft on 20th Street. From there his work was shipped to exhibitions and his secretary, Gerda Fisher, who could correspond in German, typed and kept his files. Alexander's work still had its best reception in Germany, where his old friend Dr. Wiese had encouraged Archipenko exhibitions in the fifties and acted as an intermediary with German museums as he had done in the prewar period. Stirred by the success of the 1960 show of sixty-eight sculptures that toured Germany, Dr. Wiese had helped arrange an Archipenko touring retrospective of drawings to begin in Saarbrücken in June 1962 and travel on to Mannheim and finish in Hagen. Dr. Wiese agreed to write the introduction for the catalogue. Alexander also secured future exhibitions in Switzerland, Italy, and Canada. Ferdinand Eckhardt, director of the Winnipeg Art Gallery, announced the agreement by their board of trustees to an exhibition of Archipenko's work in January 1962. The exhibition was cosponsored by the Ukrainian Alpha Omega Women's Alumnae organization. In addition, Alexander's new dealers in Switzerland not only proposed a retrospective at their gallery, but also commissioned a portfolio of lithographs with their master printer in St. Gallen at Erker-Presse and made sure that it was well-subscribed.

In a way, preparing new variants of early pieces for the next Perls show also supported Alexander's determination to create entirely new sculptures cast in bronze editions which were not variants of past works. All new and distinguishable from his early European periods, *Kimono* (fig. 53), *Tapering Figure* (fig. 54), *Linear Oriental* (fig. 55), and *Queen of Sheba* (fig. 56) were on his checklists for future exhibits.

Queen of Sheba was a particularly complicated construction. It was not often that Alexander worked on such large figures—it was sixty-five by thirty inches—and the

Fig. 56 Alexander Archipenko, *Queen of Sheba*, 1961, bronze, 66 in. (167.6 cm), Lynden Sculpture Garden, Milwaukee, WI

armature had to be carefully planned in advance before the clay could be modeled. This work indicates Alexander's growing interest in biology and biomorphic analogies. For Alexander, art without symbolism was meaningless. *Queen of Sheba*, like *Cleopatra* (fig. 30), was symbolic of feminine identity. What he expressed in a work, whether dignity, aggression, grace, or spiritualism, was often indicated by the title.

Although he'd arranged several retrospectives which included this recent work, these pieces inspired no dealer interest. As was the case with Perls, the new work was only accepted so a museum or gallery could exhibit a retrospective which included vintage Archipenko. Alexander had to make sense of what was in front of him. His current output which had the strongest currency were his variants of early sculptures, and much of his energy during 1961 was reserved for creating new editions for the 1962 Perls show. Alexander was practical. He gave the dealers and collectors what they wanted. Instinctively, he knew that Perls was primarily an opportunist, but this in no way discouraged Alexander from preparing for a show from which both of them expected to profit. Unfortunately, not all of Alexander's business decisions were profitable—or even practical.

* * *

A tape recorder and a bottle of vodka faced each other on the clumsy square oak table as Dr. Wolodymyr Wozniak told Alexander, "I borrowed the money from one of my dying patients. Now, she's dead. The family wants the money back." As he often did, Wozniak was taping the conversation with his hero—a sort of verbal imprint of their friendship. It was the fall of 1961, and they were sitting on hard pressed oak chairs in the front room at the house on Bedford Street, which was slightly below street level. We could hear the footsteps of people passing by.

Archipenko: Fifty Creative Years, 1908–58 had recently been printed. The disturbing news that there was now no money to promote the book was revealed in a conversation when both men were sodden with vodka. Refusing to work with interested commercial publishers, Alexander had ultimately made the radical decision to self-publish *Fifty Creative Years* with Wozniak, who offered to supply the money.

Alexander's unrealistic expectations of total control had doomed the project with any professional publishing house. For five years, I'd watched deal after deal fall through, usually because of Alexander's insistence that he alone should be responsible for the final design and editing. The negotiations with Beechhurst Press broke down soon after Alexander read the contract, which called for editorial oversight. He refused to allow anyone to edit him. Although his pride was interwoven with an amazing humbleness and self-respect for his own hard work ethic, it could be interpreted as arrogance.

In a grandiose gesture, Wozniak had called his bank and given Alexander several blank checks which Alexander had used to pay for the printing. Completely unaware of his own wrongdoing in using his dying patient's money, Wozniak was most concerned about maintaining his friendship with Alexander, a relationship which he was very vain about. In his strange arrogance, Wozniak was boasting, not confessing, that the money had come from a patient and that he now had to return it to her heirs. Certain he'd done the right thing in arranging the original funding to produce the book, Alexander's patron failed to realize that using a patient's money this way was not what a doctor does.

Wozniak also seemed unconcerned that his news left Alexander with the struggle to sell the almost one thousand copies of the book himself through his mailing list, and to manage advertising and seek positive reviews on his own. While it had clearly been a mistake to self-publish with Wozniak, doing business with the Ukrainian community was like comfort food for Alexander. It was not always best for his ultimate health, but it was irresistible.

Alexander had hoped, of course, that the book—which validated his aesthetic—would also cover some debts. While Gerda hauled the luxury editions, signed and bound in Moroccan leather, to the post office to be shipped to those on the subscription list—many from the Ukrainian community—Alexander had no clear plan for selling and distributing all the books he'd printed. Even though he sent out review copies to over a dozen publications, only one review was posted—and it wasn't good. One unofficial critic was Alexander's dealer, who made it clear he was appalled by the book. Klaus Perls criticized the format, illustrations, printing, and even the paper—all of which were Alexander's unique and cost-effective choices. For Perls, the fact that the book wasn't edited and produced by a high-end art publisher devalued Archipenko. Fortunately, Alexander's financial security and career did not rest with the success of his book.

In the sole review of Alexander's book, published in September 1961 in *Arts Magazine*, Sidney Geist wrote:

> Luckily for Archipenko, his reputation does not depend on this book. Not only is it unattractive physically and indigestible intellectually, but it even manages to obscure the honorable part of that reputation by dissolving the splendid first fifteen years of his production in the vast output of the last thirty-five years.[2]

Without dwelling on the negative, Alexander moved past the news that there was no money to promote his book just as he did Geist's unfavorable critique. For Alexander, it was work as usual, which in 1961 meant producing more examples of his "splendid" early output. This was yet another decision that came with some risks and a price.

I stood behind him, the sharp spotlight blacking out everything except the surface of the drawing table. He felt my presence but continued, his immersion complete, his own presence outside of the present moment. As had become our routine, after walking Sappho and picking up gelato, I had climbed to the fourth floor to join Alexander where he spent the evenings drawing. The line he created was delicate as he held the pressure of the pencil steady, moving it without hesitation. Next to the drawing was an open book revealing the image he was intent on copying. Rather than producing variants of the drawings, he went one step further. From stashes of drawing paper—some of it slightly damaged and aged—he could simulate "vintage" paper for specific drawings—all part of his artistry. He then assigned the drawing an earlier date.

Under pressure from museums and dealers—from whom early drawings were in demand so they'd have enough material for a retrospective—Alexander attempted to go back in time, producing drawings which in certain instances came very close to self-forgeries. Drawings didn't cost much to transport or buy and were of great interest to the viewing and collecting public. Galleries such as Stangl and Im Erker, as well as museums with tight budgets, incorrectly assumed that Archipenko had a stash of early drawings which could be incorporated in the retrospective exhibitions they'd scheduled.

With his new production of early ideas, Alexander had the satisfaction of re-creating his own work, fooling the collector and dealer—who wanted only his youthful work, regardless of the conditions—and making a sale. In one of the many letters William Semcesen sent Alexander between 1956 and 1959, the Ukrainian dealer blatantly orders Alexander to "make" some early drawings. This posed no problem for Alexander; it was business as usual. Even in his early years, he repeated images that were popular. If that was what it would take to have a retrospective drawing show that included his more recent works and celebrated his fifty creative years, it was not a great leap for Alexander to re-create images circa 1960 that he first realized before 1923. Yes, it was dishonest, but in the same way that Charlie Chaplin could get nutrition out of shoelaces. Actually, it was ludicrous. One could also say that Alexander was following the ancient tradition of creating relics which people were conditioned to worship.

Thus, the dating and listings of the drawings in the catalogue and the labeling for the 1962 German drawing retrospective were confusing, if not misleading. For example, the drawings *Head/Testa* (fig. 57) and *Seated* (fig. 58) were carefully rendered in 1961 in an old notebook to simulate the original, very early sketches, and then dated as 1914 in the checklist given to the museum. Eventually they appeared under this date in the catalogues as well. The drawing *Two Bodies* (fig. 59) is signed "V.2. 1913." It was listed and illustrated in the 1962 catalogue (ill. 4) as originating in 1913. That it was probably

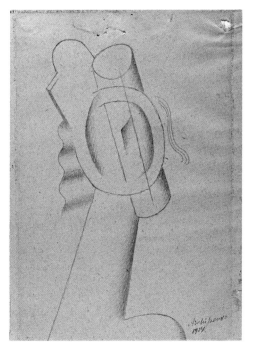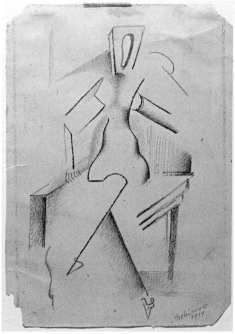

Fig. 57 Alexander Archipenko, *Head/Testa*, 1914/1961, pencil on paper (notebook), 6¹/₈ x 4⁷/₁₆ in. (15.5 x 11.2 cm), Frances Gray Collection

Fig. 58 Alexander Archipenko, *Seated*, 1961, pencil on paper, 6¹/₈ x 4³/₈ in. (15.5 x 11.2 cm), Frances Gray Collection

realized in 1961 was not indicated. Creating yet more confusion, the drawing *Two Figures, Zwei* (fig. 60) was listed and illustrated in the 1962 show (ill. 12) as originating in 1914. An inscription on the lower right, however, appears to say "Archipenko" and "1911." This drawing was probably also realized in 1961, which is, again, not indicated in the catalogue listing.

At the same time, using pastel and crayon with thick gouache on colored poster board that he set on a small wooden easel, Alexander also created completely new pieces for the 1962 drawing retrospective. Many of the finished drawings—for example, *Prophet and Woman* (fig. 61) and *Sketch for Queen of Sheba* (fig. 62), both dated 1961—were more like paintings, luminous with a big presence. But no dealer wanted to exhibit this current, more colorful work exclusively. Archipenko's reputation had been established by work that was created in Europe before 1923. The older drawings were easier to sell; they were quiet and referenced his early fame. There was a market for them.

Not at all conflicted about giving his public what they wanted, Alexander actually seemed to enjoy remaking old works. His grandfather had taught him to be an excellent

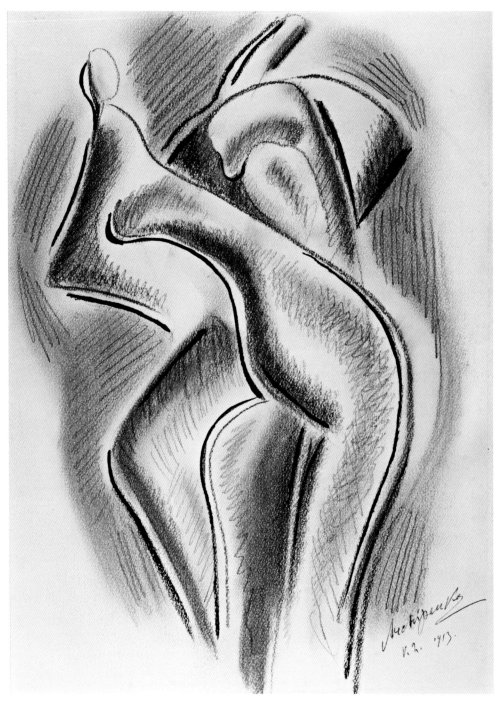

Fig. 59 Alexander Archipenko, *Two Bodies*, ca. 1961, pastel and pencil on paper, framed with glass, 10 x 14 in. (35.4 x 25.2 cm), Frances Gray Collection

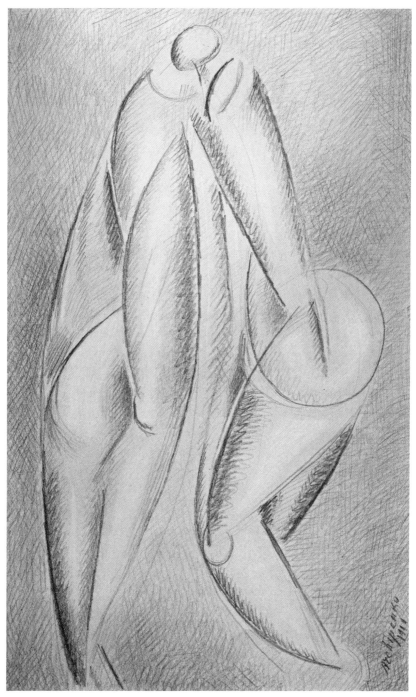

Fig. 60 Alexander Archipenko, *Two Figures, Zwei,* ca. 1961, colored pencil on paper, framed acrylic glass, 18¾ x 11¼ in. (47.5 x 28.7 cm), Frances Gray Collection

copyist when he was an adolescent convalescing. At seventy-four, Alexander's hand was very steady and his eye was sure. Certainly making sales felt good, the equivalent of "keeping the faith" and delivering an unending supply of art "relics." As we shut down for the day, sometimes at midnight, and shared the gelato I brought home, we had no idea of the problems his new old drawings might create or that his decision to include these "early drawings" on his list would require my taking a quick trip to Germany within weeks of his death.

Meanwhile, Alexander's life wasn't only twelve-hour workdays. Once a month, when we were in New York, we'd get dressed up, spread a generous buffet dinner, and fill the house with guests. People enjoyed our parties because they were so informal and the guest list was always unpredictable. In fact, the list eventually included my parents.

* * *

When I walked into my aunt Rosella's very pink hat shop on Madison Avenue, she welcomed me with open arms, congratulating me on my marriage. For Rosella, marriage was something you did many times; she and her two sisters had married at least eight times in total and had only one unmarried, sad grown daughter between them. For Aunt Rosella, nothing was sacred. This included parental love, male intelligence, and female cupidity. Family members either admired her extravagant style and attitude or kept their distance. I loved her.

While I waited for my mother, Rosella asked me to try on hats. Her hats were flattering collages of what she could sell to the Upper East Side at exorbitant prices. It was like playing in a dollhouse until my mother arrived and whisked me away with the gift of a new mink turban on my head.

Mother wasn't yet ready to congratulate me on my marriage, but her invitation to meet at Rosella's for lunch and shopping was part of a larger plan. When my father made a point of picking my mother up at my new house, they both accepted my invitation to come in. Although they hardly sat down and departed before Alexander arrived home, they were taking a peek—sniffing out how bad it could be. The feedback was in my father's expression. He had neither his usual grin nor his less frequent smile. The first floor of the house was too dark for him, and I could tell he was unimpressed by the modest furnishings. It made him feel the same way as if I were wearing a black shirt as opposed to a pastel dress. Feelings were always written on his face. Nevertheless, when they left, my parents accepted an invitation to our next party. In the safe setting of a crowd, they would visit me with my new husband for the first time. They didn't want to lose me.

Always interested in keeping my father happy, my mother called the day of the party, suggesting that I wear something "bright."

Fig. 61 Alexander Archipenko, *Prophet and Woman*, 1961, pastel and gouache on poster board, matted, 26½ x 21¼ in. (71 x 56 cm), Frances Gray Collection

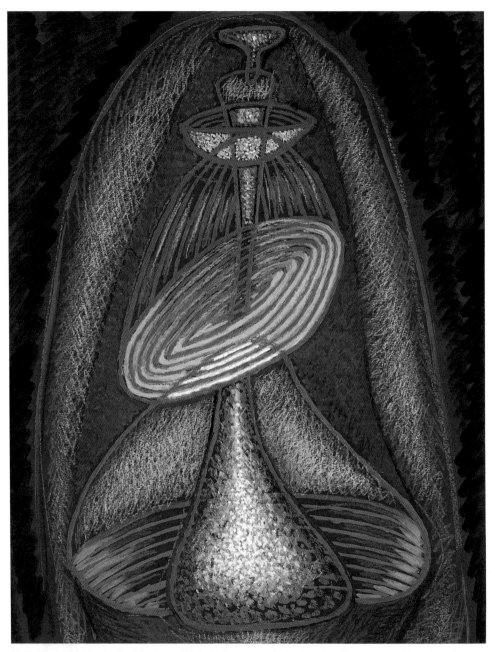

Fig.62 Alexander Archipenko, *Sketch for Queen of Sheba*, 1961, tempera and colored pencils on blue poster board, framed, 22 x 28 in. (84.4 x 69 cm), Frances Gray Collection

Alexander combed what was left of his hair over his bald pate and powdered his nose. Tonight he wanted to look as good as possible. Surveying himself in the mirror, he could see me peering at him from behind. Wrinkles were there—his, not mine. Whole muscle groups had atrophied from an undiagnosed stroke.

He turned around and faced me. His hooded eyes still revealed the cool blue he was born with. "What are you doing with this old dog?"

I made no response to his question, instead modeling my dress for the party. "Alexander, just please take a look at what I'm wearing."

Searching through my wardrobe that morning, I had chosen, perhaps spitefully, to wear the bright red satin dress which Alexander liked so much. It was made from material he had brought back for me from Switzerland, with a Greek necklace sewn into its neckline. The necklace had been purchased at a street market in Greece without a clasp and missing some links. The dress was definitely over the top, in the wrong direction. It was also a statement that I wanted to please my husband, not my parents. Alexander happily approved, forgetting the image of himself in the mirror—or perhaps imagining himself from a different time.

The clean Chinese laundry smell of Alexander's shirt was still there. It had been over five years since I first took a whiff. Now he was mine. We were married and having a domestic moment—a couple about to host a dinner party and getting dressed for the event. I can still smell the face powder, the shirt, and the air current from Bedford Street as we headed downstairs to greet our guests. We forgot about wrinkles; they weren't mine and we both disowned his.

In spite of the awkward formality which my parents projected, Alexander welcomed them with warmth at the entrance of our home. It was their first meeting with Alexander since our marriage over a year earlier. While my father remained noncommittal and kept his ground during the evening, soon Alexander and my mother were charming one another. By the end of the evening, my father had difficulty dragging her away.

Tonight's dinner party included everyone from the composer Edgard Varèse to a young art historian, a sophisticated collector, our plumber—whom Alexander had invited when he ran into him on the street—and a few of Alexander's old girlfriends. Throughout his life, Alexander had developed many romantic liaisons. Some were more memorable than others, but he always honored the remaining friendships. He had a sort of fan club of intelligent "older women," who often dragged their husbands along. I met and liked several of these friends; they were, of course, always much older than I, but also much younger than Alexander and always very kind to me.

On the other hand, even though he was Alexander's contemporary, Varèse seemed very much older because he was rather grumpy and bossed me around, thinking nothing of asking me to go down two flights of stairs to bring him an ice cube or some salt. Varèse had been one of Alexander's sponsors when Alexander came to the United States in 1923. They hadn't been in contact for many years, however, until I accidentally met the composer over our garden wall after a great ruckus involving my barking Dalmatian attempting to leap up our peach tree at a snarling cat at the top. Explaining that he was a client of our neighbor, who repaired musical instruments, Varèse handed me his calling card. Now that he was back in contact with Alexander, he was permanently on our invitation list. Whenever he attended, however, I appreciated Alexander so much more. Varèse's treatment of me may have been generational, but my husband would never think of asking me to wait on him.

The house was perfect for socializing because guests could move around. Actually, they had little choice, since there were never enough chairs and most of the space was on the staircase. I remember a tremendous amount of good feeling when I slowed down enough to catch sight of my mother chatting with the collector and my father going back to the buffet table. For the most part, however, I loved watching Alexander have a good time. When I first met him, he seemed so withdrawn and at times quite sad, and now he was welcoming both old friends and new acquaintances, including my parents.

Perhaps because of Archipenko's obvious fame and respectful manners, this party marked a great change in attitude on the part of my family. We were now all practical and willing to work it out. By the second or third visit, once my brother and his wife had come to the house, my father was starting to take on an attitude that hinted at proprietorship, introducing himself without self-consciousness as my father.

That my parents traveled to St. Gallen the next year to be present at the opening celebration of Alexander's exhibition proved we were taking a good path together. As time went by, we enhanced each other's lives. Eventually Alexander trusted that my parents would be supportive of me and our shared goals when he passed. Ironically, the healing of our estrangement began when my mother came to imagine me as acceptably glamorous. An added dividend for my family was that they could take on boasting rights about their sophisticated daughter, who was an artist in her own right and was married to a world-famous artist.

But something was changing for me. Any glamour I had came from my husband, not from my own work as an artist.

* * *

Because my studio on Bedford Street was on the top floor of a narrow town house, it was a hike to bring up supplies and also to remove debris such as wood chips or plaster waste molds. As a result, I limited myself to modeling small sculptures and making drawings. But once I was settled in the studio for the day, it was my nest, a place that was mine and where I sometimes remained by myself for four to six hours at a time. Even Alexander only came up if he wanted to use the space in the evening to work.

This is what Alexander wanted for me. Even on the most dreary days, it was always bright. Nothing blocked the light, and the small peach tree in the garden was just enough to hint at abundance. When not lying on the studio floor next to me, Sappho was out in the garden, looking for cat activity and overseen by me. My view from the fourth floor also included the city, which I could either avoid or include in my focus from time to time. It all felt rich.

In truth, I remember the space more than the work I did in it. My focus was no longer preparing work for an exhibition. The pieces that went to Europe for shows in Frankfurt and London were the small castings which had been in the exhibition at the Delacorte Gallery—ready to go and easy to transport.

While I found great pleasure being in my studio, I went there only after my chores maintaining the household were done. My life had become busy with a new type of responsibility. Perhaps it was the domestic aspect of my life which was subtly inhibiting me. Whatever I created at Bedford Street was never shown and, for that reason, not photographed. Nor do I remember the work. Producing more small sculptures was automatic, but left me feeling as if I were occupied with "busywork." This sweet studio exercised my agility as I endlessly tread water. Alexander was the artist, the one preparing for a major year of exhibits.

Chapter Twelve
A Renaissance Year

Winnipeg in January was almost surreal. Behind the flat, serene landscape, danger lurked in the form of cold. When we woke up the first morning, we looked out our hotel window to a crystal blue sky. In a deep, quiet voice, Alexander ordered our breakfast and then held my hand as we stared in amazement at the blueness of the sky, so at odds with the bone-chilling temperature. We agreed that the sky looked too Mediterranean for it to be so cold—as if colors could really be honest in predicting temperature. Looking down at the street, I noticed a dog not moving; he had been frozen stiff on an evening stroll. When I unwrapped a bouquet of red roses given to me at a ladies' luncheon a few days later, they'd turned black from the cold during a short walk from the car to the hotel.

We'd come to Winnipeg for an Archipenko retrospective exhibition. At the airport, we were greeted by the mayor and Dr. Ferdinand Eckhardt, director of the Winnipeg Art Gallery. Our two motorcycle escorts, whom I assumed to be Canadian Mounties, were unable to open the frozen locked trunk of our VIP limousine to retrieve our luggage. Throughout our stay, we were supervised by the more experienced locals, who instructed us to expose our warmly layered bodies to the elements for only ten minutes at a time—and to be sure to time it. It was still, with no wind, a white end-of-the-world place. I understood for the first time why white has been the color of mourning in certain cultures.

Although I hardly remember the forty-six piece retrospective exhibition at the Winnipeg Art Gallery, sponsored by the Ukrainian Alpha Omega Women's Alumnae organization, I do remember being treated like visiting celebrities. Manitoba's lieutenant governor officiated at the opening, during which Alexander was made an honorary citizen of the province. Maybe it was the dooming sense of isolation from the intense cold that made the hospitality feel so warm. When I mentioned the local zoo to my guide, to my delight she took me to see real polar bears, who were comfortably lounging in the minus forty degree weather, white fur glistening against white snow. When they moved, it was with a languor which seemed tropical.

Back at the hotel after a day of separate activities, Alexander and I had no time to compare our experiences; we had to rush off to a cocktail party and on to a collector's home for dinner. Eckhardt and his wife had arranged for us to meet with local art patrons who, along with the Ukrainian community, had made the exhibition possible. Very knowledgeable about Archipenko's work and history, these supporters were thrilled that the retrospective exhibition had come to Winnipeg.

In fact, in 1962, everyone seemed thrilled with Alexander. The Winnipeg show was the second of several high-profile exhibitions in North America and Europe during what was a renaissance year for Alexander. A week before the opening in Winnipeg, Archipenko had returned to a prestigious place in the New York art scene with a solo show of eighteen bronzes at the Perls Galleries. Also scheduled were the drawing retrospective in its three-museum tour in Germany during the summer; a one-man show at the Galerie Grosshennig in Düsseldorf, which would sell a major work to the Centre Pompidou; and a major exhibition in St. Gallen, Switzerland, in November. It was also during this year that Archipenko was elected a member of America's National Institute of Arts and Letters.

Suddenly, Alexander was newsworthy. "Archipenko Has a Comeback" was the subheadline in a March 1962 Life magazine lead article.[1] In addition, Time featured an illustrated piece commenting: "To speak of Alexander Archipenko is, for many, to speak of a ghost—an artist whose glories are in the past and who only haunts the present. Yet no ghost could be more lively. This week an Archipenko retrospective will open at Manhattan's Perls Galleries, and another show will head for a tour of Canada. Archipenko has always been an innovator; at 74, he still is."[2]

The Winnipeg show was the kind of event that Alexander was most pleased to travel for, even though the temperature was minus forty degrees. He felt his best when he had an appreciative audience. Aside from several important sales to enthusiastic collectors and some beautiful memories, traveling to Winnipeg erased my thoughts of much of the previous week in New York. We had flown to Winnipeg five days after the less than celebratory opening of the new bronze exhibit at the Perls Galleries.

Attending my first New York opening as Alexander's wife, I was also part of the show, looking and feeling grand in my mink turban from Aunt Rosella, which matched the mink collar of the nutria fur coat Alexander had given me. The show itself wasn't an event that I remember in any detail, however. It merges in my memory with the other openings at the Perls Galleries. Although well reviewed, with some additions and changes, it was clearly commercial in purpose: a repeat of the intent of the 1959 bronze show. Dolly Perls and the staff took turns with the counter, and she let it be known that attendance was "adequate."

Fig. 63 Alexander Archipenko, *Festive*, 1961, bronze, 28 x 18 x 10¼ in. (71.1 x 45.7 x 26 cm), Frances Gray Collection

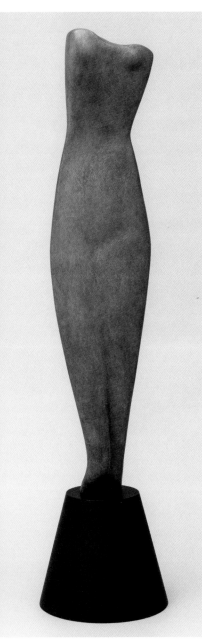

In reality, Dolly and Klaus were happy to see everyone leave. Their work happened mostly in private, before or after the general public. Klaus Perls was essentially a business man. The collectors he cultivated understood this—and they had confidence that their money was well invested. In turn, Alexander appreciated Perls's connections, which were outside his usual radar. Always a bit rough around the edges—even when he took the time to polish up—Alexander was often more comfortable rolling up his sleeves and cleaning out a drainage ditch or talking with academics than he was socializing with the Madison Avenue art elite.

As for business, Alexander cooperated fully with Perls. The money was important to him. He was enjoying some financial success and wanted it to continue.

Unfortunately, Alexander's unique new works—the six sculptures he had created and cast in bronze editions during the previous year, in 1961—didn't tempt collectors. Although *Time* mentioned these works in a positive context, describing Archipenko as "an innovator," these pieces, including *Queen of Sheba* (fig. 56), *Festive* (fig. 63), *Kimono* (fig. 53), and *Linear Oriental* (fig. 55), were not appreciated and—although exhibited occasionally over the years—never became a strong part of the market. As had happened with the sculpto-paintings, they were at odds with what was expected, and often noted as "eccentric."

Again, what attracted attention and sales at the show were the ten bronzes which were pre-1920 in conception, six of which were new variants, conceived to be bronze editions. Perls could also stand behind the 1935 *Torso in Space* (fig. 46). Because a slightly different-sized variant of this work had found a buyer at the 1959 Perls exhibition, there was interest. The other torso in the show, the 1936 *Hollywood Torso* (fig. 64), was also desirable. Both were identifiable as signature Archipenko works, aggressively beautiful in their elegance.

Although Alexander gave only minimal attention to the issues of authenticity which were already surfacing about his work, he did have time to retaliate further against his old nemesis Estorick. In a letter sent to Perls about this time, justifying his part in the showdown with Archipenko, Estorick referred to *Statuette*: "Well over a year ago, the three copies of an original piece which Andrew Goeritz has, were given to Mr. Goeritz. This was done at the instigation of Archipenko and Goeritz has obviously destroyed them. For Archipenko at this stage to say that he doesn't believe they were destroyed is an absurdity."[3] Later, when Alexander was sent a photo of one of the London casts of *Geometric Statuette* by the Baltimore Museum of Art, he informed the curator: "I regret to inform you that this is not my original and it looks like a very bad cast and did not come from my studio."[4] We have no way of knowing if this was actually one of the bronzes which he had approved and been paid for. Today at least six and possibly more copies of this piece are in circulation.

But Alexander didn't dwell on these matters. He was happy. The variants were attracting sales and headlines. As we headed into the summer of 1962, the obstacles which had plagued him when we first met—his flagging reputation, his sadness over Angelica, and his heavy financial burdens—were dissolving. Alexander was starting his life over—with me.

* * *

One night as Alexander passed through my studio to the little room in the back for another evening of work, he paused by a small sculpture sitting separately on one of my stands. He recognized that my eleven-year-old nephew Jeffrey had come back with me after I took him to MoMA to see a photography exhibition. As he often did, Jeffrey had played with Plasticine until it was time for him to catch his train back to Westchester.

Alexander stared at the tiny sculpture for several minutes. He was thinking. Finally, he said, "Frances, do you want to have a child?"

Taken off guard, my response was slow in coming. It was the first time in Alexander's life that he had said he would like to have a child. He'd never wanted to have children with Angelica. Involved in the demimonde as a young woman, Angelica had a daughter who remained behind when she left Germany with Archipenko in 1923. Her first husband was in the theater, and in the early 1920s in Europe, the lives of artists could be willfully undomesticated. Children were known to suffer collateral damage. This, I believe, was the case with Angelica's daughter.

Perhaps it was the frequent visits from my nephew, now that he was old enough to travel alone, that led Alexander to think about the possibility of our having our own child. Infants were cute when they were not demanding, but it wasn't a stage that particularly attracted Alexander. On the other hand, Jeffrey was always very charming and generous in his demonstrative imitation of adulthood. For instance, he loved to treat me to an ice cream with his allowance.

Alexander's desire for a child may have also been the natural outcome of the nesting instinct which developed once he had enough financial security to buy the house on Bedford Street. Somehow during our travels we'd accumulated enough African and ethnic art to begin furnishing the house, and Alexander loved to bring me extravagant gifts for our new home. One day a huge polar bearskin rug arrived and became a centerpiece in the house. The gifts also included a mirrored vanity he'd constructed in his studio with painted plywood and piano hinges. It was splinter free, but clearly not the work of a cabinetmaker. All of these offerings had been his way of nest-building, perhaps to counteract all the traveling he had recently done and which was still ahead for us.

Whatever the reason, Alexander's decision was a testament to his happiness in our life together. Our age difference reduced the friction of competitiveness that seemed to often occur among peers. Our unconditional acceptance of each other came without much effort, and our differences were so unchanging that an argument or a disagreement was a waste of energy. Winning or losing didn't occur. I don't remember having to negotiate. We were able to look at things together; whoever wanted something just got it. It was never a conventional "couple thing." Perhaps that was the key which made it possible for me to love him. I felt fully protected from domination, manipulation, and retribution—those qualities which were part of my childhood.

I felt a surge of emotion which came from a new place in my being. Alexander had no family except for me, and his desire to have a child with me bound us together in a new way that was many-faceted. It meant that he trusted me and that our relationship had intent beyond the moment—the clear intent of legacy. I was reminded of a comment in a letter from Dr. Wiese: "It is so wonderful that you and your wife Frances are now freshly working together."[5]

As the air turned warm and it was time to head for Europe again, we began to imagine that a child could be our next experience together.

Alexander no longer spoke about my fulfilling a revival of his early promise as an artist, however. At seventy-four, he was still intact, renowned as a modern master, and working on new creative projects. He was reliving his early fame himself.

* * *

When we arrived for the June 9 opening in Saarbrücken of the touring drawing retrospective, it was the German version of la dolce vita with everybody, including their teenage children, drinking up a storm. In 1962, Germany was once again the country most receptive to Archipenko's work, as the German museums continued the project of rebuilding all they'd lost. The first evening began with champagne served nonstop and many courses of food which were carefully served by scrupulously groomed waiters. I couldn't see Alexander at the long table, as he was surrounded by what were probably a lot of state officials all dressed in black tie. I was dressed for the formality in a simple A-line which was very "Camelot."

Dr. Rudolf Bornschein, the director in Saarbrücken, welcomed us with carte blanche to live and work in separate studios for as many months as we wanted in Schloss Halberg, a castle owned by the state and used to house VIPs. This was no musty old building. All the furniture was Eames, and bright primary colors were de rigueur. Alexander was anxious to get back to work in New York, however, and refused the offer.

Before the year ended, we returned to Europe one last time—now to Switzerland—for the November 1962 opening of Alexander's solo exhibit of sculptures, drawings, and watercolors at the Galerie Im Erker in St. Gallen. The actual vernissage, which my parents attended, was private and included a dinner in a rented castle: a drafty ancient wooden structure with a moat. After my parents left, we stayed on and Alexander worked at the printers completing a commission for a portfolio of lithographs, *Les Formes Vivantes*.

It's only now, in going through the correspondence between Alexander and the two Im Erker partners, that I realize how many unfortunate difficulties and misunderstandings were mounting as Alexander planned to send work from this show on to his large retrospective in Rome the next spring. Even though everyone from both sides was well-intentioned and generally respectful, the same problems were emerging: the concept of the "variant" and confused or missing cast numbers.

Writing to Archipenko about the current St. Gallen show in a letter dated December 14, 1962, one partner, Jürg Janett, spelled out his concerns:

> The collector who bought the "Flat Torso" at the opening of the exhibition has renounced this purchase when we were obliged to tell him of the existence of 24 copies of this work. It will generally be difficult for us to sell works of such a great number of casts. Mainly in Switzerland the collectors are very "sensible" in this point.
>
> The "versions" and "enlargements" of earlier sculptures are looked upon with the same distrust. We shall therefore have some difficulties in placing copies of the enlarged "Seated black concave" [sic].
>
> At the same time we should be thankful to you if you could let us know which one of the works shown in our gallery are originals and which one are "versions". We owe our collectors full information about this point. As a matter of fact we have also been asked for this information by some German and Swiss museums.[6]

His Swiss dealers had a point. Alexander hadn't taken edition numbers very seriously in his early production, and now the creation of variants and new versions made the issue ever more confusing. Granted, it was difficult for Alexander to keep track of the casts he was producing and selling through such a large number of dealers, including Klaus Perls in New York, Gerald Cramer in Geneva, William Semcesen in Norway, and others in Germany and elsewhere. Sometimes the finisher made a mistake in the cast insignia and this wasn't caught in time. Sometimes it was just too much juggling, what with the delivery from the foundry, shipping overseas, and private sales directly from the studio.

There were also problems around consistency of pricing in regard to the coming show in Rome, because any works which were not sold in St. Gallen were to be sent to that show. In addition, although they had sold enough works to encourage an ongoing relationship, there was no resolution with regard to Im Erker's full representation of Archipenko.

As we finally headed home, Alexander never mentioned his dealers' concerns. It would seem he left to history questions that had to do with marketing and authenticating. Right now he was receiving an enthusiastic reception throughout North America and Europe and wanted to get home to continue preparing for his major retrospective in Rome.

* * *

While Alexander experienced a renaissance in 1962, I was experiencing a sense of restlessness. Trying to be productive in my fourth-floor studio on Bedford Street caused me to be self-conscious and drift away from my projects. I started to do more drawings using color, but it all felt stale. I was probably doing too much of the same thing.

My workday no longer progressed as it had in the beginning, when everything was fresh and a bit of a lark. As it often had over our seven years together, my work felt like a spin-off of Alexander's expectations. Underneath, something was fermenting which I sensed, but denied. Before long, I started to feel constricted, like a bird in a cage, as I looked out the window at the garden below or at the street in the front of the house, waiting for the evening when Alexander would return. Eventually I came to recognize that I didn't take myself seriously as an artist. It was my life with Alexander that I took seriously.

Although we never conceived a child together, when I did give birth to a son many years after Alexander's death, I named him Alexander. It was in a different way that I was to become the exclusive guardian of Archipenko's legacy.

Fig. 65 Alexander Archipenko, *Walking Torso*, 1963, plaster, 14¹/₁₀ x 4³/₅ x 6⁹/₁₀ in. (35.8 x 11.8 x 17.5 cm), Saarland Museum, Saarbrücken, Germany

Fig. 66 Alexander Archipenko, *King Solomon*, 1963, bronze, 26¼ x 9 in. (66.7 x 22.9 cm), Smithsonian American Art Museum, Washington, DC

Fig. 67 Alexander Archipenko with *King Solomon* plaster, 1963, Archipenko Foundation, Bearsville, NY

Once again, he surprised me. As 1962 came to a close—without telling me—Alexander put a sizable, nonrefundable deposit on a space in Chelsea that he planned to establish as a dedicated museum for his work. In Paris, he'd looked at his friends who had stayed in one place and thus had the protection and stability provided by the French government and its municipal museums. Alexander's relationship with the New York art world had shifted again, and he had no reassurance about what would happen to his work after he was gone. The internationally known sculptor with an Eastern European background was now wary of the urbane and sophisticated personalities controlling the market forces. Stepping back from the commercial politics that governed art in the 1960s, Alexander recognized the practical need for a venue to store, protect, and show his work after his death.

He envisioned this space ultimately as a museum which would keep his work on exhibition in perpetuity. In the interim, it would be an independent place for the bronze finisher, thus keeping Alexander's own studio noise-free and clear of dust. Even better, there would be no need to leave the working plasters at the foundry once the bronze was delivered. While he understood his importance, Alexander—moving as he did from place to place—hadn't cared for his early work adequately in the past. Now everything would be returned and stored in Chelsea.

Listening to his plans over our evening meal, I thought about what it all meant. I continued to digest the news as I washed up the dishes, and then suggested we take Sappho for her evening walk together and stop for gelato. I didn't question that part of my role was to save his work and pull it into the future when he was gone. Settled in the house on Bedford Street, truly married, we were pledged to each other's welfare. But would it be my job to run a museum? I was hardly a fundraiser, particularly well-connected, or experienced in the ways of the world. The real problem was that I didn't feel secure about making these decisions. While it felt good to be given that trust, I had no idea how this responsibility would define my future.

Bleecker Street was still animated with storekeepers starting to close down for the day as we settled at a table. Alexander waited for me to speak first.

I met his eyes. "Whatever you plan, if I'm involved, we need to write everything down. And we need to use my family lawyer."

A week later, in front of the lawyer, I broke the news to Alexander that I didn't know how to do what he most wanted and that I was afraid that if I tried, I'd fail. In the end, after our meeting, we were of one mind. The solution was that in his proper last will and testament I would be able to administer the donation of his models to an appropriate institution. I wouldn't have to open a museum.

Meanwhile, Alexander had installed his finisher in the new building and continued working days at the 20th Street loft, where he created another nude torso for his repertoire, the *Walking Torso* (fig. 65). Although this piece was small and in bronze, it had a touch of his new metamorphic style, as did the 1957 *Lying Horizontal Figure* (fig. 38), which referenced his earlier Floating and Reclining Torsos.

In addition, the image of King Solomon had been on Alexander's mind ever since he struggled with the first version a year earlier, finally destroying it in frustration. His *Queen of Sheba* (fig. 56) needed a consort. Whereas that sculpture paid tribute to a certain kind of woman and her mystery, this companion piece was a meditation on a mature male character. One might say that through the image of *King Solomon* (fig. 66), Alexander was free-associating on wealth, wisdom, and women as he entered his mid-seventies. By the next spring, Alexander would approve the first bronze cast—which was approximately twenty-seven inches—sending it to Munich for his 1964 exhibition. He also created a black-and-white plaster model (fig. 67) for enlargement as a contribution to the Enzo Pagani sculpture garden in Castellanza.

Most days during the winter of 1962 and 1963, however, the noise and dust from Alexander's studio came from carpentry. He had crates to build for his statues and for the huge display placards which had to be shipped for the exhibit in Rome. It was an enormous task that he accomplished with a steady and focused energy, building every crate himself. In the evenings, he remained focused on the Rome show. When he wasn't making drawings, he was working on a long table set up in my studio, creating informational placards with photographs of his early output.

Unfortunately, no amount of energy could guarantee that the crates with the work would arrive at the exhibition site.

Chapter Thirteen
Finishing Touches

With the lights dimmed and the high windows draped, the Palazzo Barberini—where Archipenko's solo retrospective would be installed in Rome—began to feel haunted. Our footsteps echoed each day as we hiked up the oval Borromini marble staircase and walked through this pillared, cavernous hall imagining how all the work and explanatory placards would look in the space which was allotted to the Archipenko exhibit. The building was quite grand, and the circular staircase up to the exhibition space was breathtaking. The catalogue included an essay by Gino Severini.

The most pressing question was the whereabouts of the work itself. When we arrived in Rome, we were told that the crates with the sculptures and placards hadn't arrived but were "somewhere" in customs and needed to be "released." The information offered was cryptic. We were told someone needed to be paid, but it wasn't clear who or why. Every morning, we'd walk down the hill from our very pleasant hotel at the top of the Spanish Steps to the Palazzo Barberini and be told the same story by the director, Dr. Giovanni Sangiorgi, and his assistant, who greeted us with a smile and a shrug. As the days wore on, everything was at a complete standstill.

Alexander was concerned about who would make the temporary walls and stands in time for the opening deadline to be met. To us, this felt like a serious situation, but we discovered it was normal for Italy. Dr. Sangiorgi's assistant scurried about attempting to look busy, usually by himself, as he waited for our arrival each day. When at least a week had passed, Alexander became extremely frustrated. We decided I would go to the American consulate and ask for help while Alexander proceeded to the exhibition space—just in case something had changed.

Although I didn't have an appointment, much to my surprise, the official at the consulate was extremely helpful, making phone calls on our behalf. It seems that we had unwittingly called someone's bluff. In our naïveté, we did not realize that a tip was expected; nor did we know who was to give or get it. When the consulate's office got word to the bureaucrats in charge that they'd have to release the works from customs, everything finally arrived at the exhibition site. Now the installation could begin. That is, after the crates were unpacked.

Alexander made a point of immediately taking off his jacket and rolling up his sleeves. As the packing material flew in all directions, Dr. Sangiorgi's baffled assistant insisted he was getting workers to do this. Apparently it was déclassé for him to do any physical work. I helped by checking the works as they came out of the crates, which entailed making little sketches of each piece—the equivalent of a condition report. In the end, Alexander was concerned about the crates being in good shape for the return shipping, so we did most of the unpacking ourselves, being careful to retain all the packing material. So it went for days, with a lone workman to help us.

Because he had another part-time job as well—as journalist for the Vatican newspaper—Dr. Sangiorgi was rarely to be found on the premises except around midday. Then he'd invite us to his apartment for a large meal with his wife and university-age children, who still came home for lunch every day. When the meal ended, everyone disappeared to take a nap. Life began again at around four o'clock in the afternoon, with the workday sometimes ending as late as nine. We'd head back to the hotel from the exhibition site just as Rome really came alive. The streets and cafés remained vibrant till after midnight, and the sounds of howling feral cats and cars and motorcycles revving up went on all night.

With long lunch breaks and many misunderstandings, the installation of the works was a slow process. Directing professional carpenters and installers, Alexander first laboriously put together the corridor of images, mostly photographs, which recorded the history of his artistic career and led into the actual exhibition. These images were of early work which was no longer available for exhibition. Next came a large hallway of wall dividers on which were hung sixty-six drawings, some of them sketches for the sculptures on display. For example, in keeping with his goal to show the evolution of his work, Alexander exhibited *Nine Work Sketches for Sculpture II* (fig. 24) from 1930 (seven of these nine sketches developed into sculptures) and several other groupings to illustrate his method of working from sketches to realized sculptures. Fifty-four sculptures were installed in the open rooms.

All of this took more than a bit of doing. When we arrived the day before the official opening, we were relieved to find all the stands up, elegantly draped with fabric—there'd been no time to paint—and the temporary walls standing with the drawings and placards on the floor for Alexander's approval before being mounted. The installers must have been at it all night after we left.

Extreme formality presided as Alexander was congratulated by the mayor of Rome, with Dr. Sangiorgi and other officials hovering in the background. There was an almost

Fig. 68 Alexander Archipenko, *Saluto! alla Grande alla Bella alla eternal Roma!*, 1962, collage, 27 3/4 x 23 3/8 in. (70.6 x 59.3 cm), Frances Gray Collection

theatrical liveliness in Rome, a vibrancy which was lacking in Paris, where Alexander's connections and reputation had yet to finalize a contract with a dealer or museum. As a heartfelt tribute to Rome, he designed the exhibition poster in which he signifies: *Saluto! alla Grande alla Bella alla eternal Roma!* (fig. 68).

By the time we returned to the hotel after the opening, I was spent. Now that the stress of the installation and official launch was over, I was happy to stare at a blank wall in private. Alexander also needed quiet time. Soon enough there would be more openings. A portion of the exhibition later went to Milan and the rest to the Galerie Stangl in Munich.

In retrospect I understand that I was discreetly not included when Alexander made a trip to Milan to plan a retrospective at the Centro Culturale San Fedele. Perhaps because the contrast in our ages was difficult for the sponsors—devout members of the Catholic Church—to digest, the curator, a young priest involved with contemporary art, must have believed my presence might distract from the work and his mission to introduce less conventional art. Whatever the reason, I stayed in Rome for the day. Over the past year, however, I'd been welcomed, interviewed, and photographed at Alexander's multiple exhibitions.

A revived international stature also meant facing the ever-shifting currents in the politics of art. Like water, the art world flowed naturally but unpredictably. At different times, Alexander found himself moving with the current, swimming against it, or treading water. The passages were sometimes rocky, sometimes smooth, and often fast.

* * *

As our boat moved forward through the murkiness and we slid under low-hanging bridges, Alexander reminisced about the thrill of his first experience in Venice some forty years earlier, remembering how he was celebrated and in his prime. In 1920 he had been the featured artist at the twelfth Venice Biennale, his one-person show including some eighty-six works at the Russian Pavilion. Alexander had honored Venice with a sculpture called *Gondolier* (fig. 69), and his name echoed all over the city. Always one for sharing his good fortune with a woman, he'd had a glamorous blonde lover melting by his side in a gondola as the gondoliers paid him tribute by calling out his name when they came to crossings. Gliding over the water with me now, in 1963, he made it all sound thrilling: the experience of being an artist hero. That memory had remained neatly embedded in his psyche, ready to be brought forth whenever needed.

After the Rome opening, in Alexander's imagination, Venice had called again. With me as his companion, he wanted to return to the city as part of a voyage back in time. However, forty years later, the gondoliers didn't know him. Only at an international artists' hangout was Alexander recognized and treated like a celebrity.

In the four years during which we were married, our itinerary traveling in Europe had always been determined either by an existing exhibition or the possibility of one. Now we were finally tourists. As we were deposited at a very elegant hotel just off the Grand Canal and lifted our luggage over the edge of the brackish water, I saw that the lower part of the outside wall of the hotel was submerged and invisible. While we wandered through narrow streets and over bridges, the canals smelled almost pleasant in their

Fig. 69 Alexander Archipenko (1887–1964), © ARS, NY. *Gondolier*, 1914 (cast 1966), bronze, 33 x 11⅞ x 10⅛ in. (83.8 x 30.1 x 25.5 cm) including base. Gift of Frances Archipenko Gray in honor of Alfred H. Barr, Jr. The Museum of Modern Art, New York, NY, U.S.A. Digital image © The Museum of Modern Art/Licensed by SCALA/Art Resource, NY.

decadence. But I sensed a prevailing instability, with the tides of the ocean constantly creeping up and down the ancient building walls we passed, entering through crevices and leaving grimy deposits. Venice was always doing battle with stench and decay. Whenever possible, it camouflaged itself in elegance. The transient luxury of our hotel, which had once been a palace, with its almost costumed staff, was comical and cinema-like.

Although I was enchanted by Venice, I think that for Alexander our visit prompted the realization that he was very far away in time from his first experience in this city. After his huge success in 1920, Alexander's work was never again seen at the Venice Biennale. Venice had not changed, but World War I had changed the aesthetic and social/political sensibilities for future and immediate generations of international artists.

When we visited the current Venice Biennale exhibits, we paid a call on the director, who in later correspondence voiced both his respect for Alexander and his inability to include Alexander's current work in the next Biennale. Although still respected and remembered, Archipenko—being an American citizen—was now a bit off-center and at odds. The individual countries made their choices, not the director. As a nationalized American citizen who was not in any way affiliated with American Abstract Expressionism, Alexander's work was not defined by his nationality. Nor was his nationality defined by his work. One could say that he was too international to participate in an international show that needed a lot of moving parts, individual countries clearly defined by their artists. This reality added cruelly to the romance of Venice.

In Greece, our next stop, Alexander had the opportunity to reflect further on the powers that controlled these exhibitions as we visited Christos Kapralos, who had represented Greece the previous year in the Venice Biennale. An artist who admired Alexander and understood current art politics, he was also easy to like. Very disdainful of the way choices were made for the Biennale, Kapralos, when asked to submit his work, sent a photograph of a crushed sardine can as a joke. Much to our amusement, the photograph, which he showed us, was accepted along with more serious work that he'd submitted. Greece was also suffering from political repression, and Kapralos knew that if not for his own Greek nationalism and postwar commissions, he wouldn't have been representing Greece in Venice that year. In a short time, Alexander and Kapralos developed a camaraderie that took to task the Biennale selection process, trends in the art world, and American Abstract Expressionism (both artists disparaged pure abstraction as a current catchall).

While we were viewing Kapralos's work, he spontaneously suggested that Alexander should stay in Athens and share the small bronze foundry attached to his studio. It was a relatively simple operation—a shed almost hidden in the backyard on a dirt floor with basic equipment limited to one casting at a time. I could see that Alexander was touched. So typical of our experience in Greece was this instant sharing and unconditional generosity from Kapralos, who also showed us parts of Athens we might miss on our own.

As we toured the Parthenon, the heat in Athens felt brutal; the traffic fumes were even more unpleasant than in Paris or London. It was dry, and I felt dehydrated even though we both drank chilled lemon sodas in the tepid lobby before wandering out of our government-franchised hotel. Alexander wore a short-sleeved cotton shirt and I a sleeveless yellow dress with sandals, which, with all the sand and pebbles at the Acropolis, was a mistake. But it was wonderful. We were both in awe of this picture postcard come to life, especially Alexander, who had waited a lifetime to view this architectural icon and to experience his human proportions next to the columns on the high and rugged outcropping overlooking the city of Athens. As we walked back to our hotel, the clarity of the sky was pure and the air hinted at olives and thyme.

When we arrived at a small "taverna" in a village near Delphi, they refused to serve us until our driver explained that we were artists, not the usual tourists, and that we were there to celebrate my birthday away from home. A few locals darted out of the café and soon returned with musicians. Art and being an artist was always something to celebrate. As we went on to the isle of Crete—with introductions from Christos Kapralos—Alexander took pleasure in reading the signs in Cyrillic, the alphabet he learned as a child. No longer in Europe, he was now closer to his true emotional roots, the Greek Orthodox Church, his early Ukrainian background, and the icon painting of his childhood. Seeing the restoration of Knossos, the Minoan palace, took Alexander further back in art history as he fully appreciated this site where the first advanced pre-Christian civilization arose.

Even though it was only May, the bright sun reflecting off the sea did its damage as we explored the island. My shoulders peeled all the way back to New York.

That November, Alexander took what would be his last trip to Europe, for the opening of the Milan show. When he returned to Bedford Street on December 5, 1963, all was well and balanced for Alexander—financially, personally, and professionally. It was the height of his revived fame, and we experienced it together. Soon, though, we would experience something much darker.

* * *

Working on a new plaster polychrome version of *King Solomon* in the two months before his death, Alexander was calm and strong, his hands dynamically poised in a virile attitude. He had returned home exhausted and with some flu-like symptoms from the trip to Milan, but he was unwilling to rest. Although neither of us knew it, this was to be his last project. His focus was relentless as he fought fatigue and discomfort. Although he said he was "very tired" from overwork, Alexander rarely complained and simply became even more driven. At the same time, I also sensed his slow withdrawal, which began affecting our relationship in subtle ways.

As I admitted to myself that he was fading, I made arrangements with a taxi driver to take Alexander to his studio on 20th Street every day and then to bring him home. His greatest wish was to work and remain active. My greatest fear was that he would be stricken when alone. As long as he was working or thinking about work, he avoided any attention to his growing frailties. He was also approaching the final steps in taking title to the new building, still hoping that it would eventually serve as a museum for his work.

By mid-February 1964, it was cold and Alexander was tiring more quickly. But he continued putting the finishing touches on his polychrome version of *King Solomon*. This latest version was to be enlarged and installed as a monument in a sculpture park outside Milan by the collector Enzo Pagani. Alexander unrealistically imagined the eventual enlargement as a colossus on the scale of the Statue of Liberty. Just two weeks before he died, he completed the piece—the last sculpture created by Archipenko—and shipped it to Italy.

Our deepest bond still was his work, and he continued working and planning until the end; everything else was subordinate. It was almost the way a functional couple might raise a child until it gained independence—intuitively and mutually taking care of its needs. His work became our child and his legacy. Archipenko, a colossus as human, was failing.

Jumping into the taxi with him one morning, I gave the taxi driver instructions to change the destination from the 20th Street studio to Columbia Presbyterian Hospital. We were going to see a cardiologist who'd been recommended by a member of my family. By counting the number of nitroglycerin tablets remaining in the medicine bottle next to his nightstand, I'd discovered that Alexander was naively and discreetly treating his endangered heart with his own regimen of pills. He was determined to avoid hospitalization—his experience with Angelica's long illnesses and institutionalization disallowed any discussion of the issue.

Up to this point, Alexander had been treated by a primary care physician from the Ukrainian community. Alarmed by the amount and variety of medication he was consuming, I tricked him into getting a second opinion from a specialist. After reading the labels on all of Alexander's medications, Dr. Cooper discarded them in the trash can in front of us, saying they were of no help. He prescribed just one medication.

The doctor was discreet in what he said to Alexander, who adamantly refused to be hospitalized but agreed to stay in bed for his flu-like symptoms. He took me aside, however, and explained that my husband's heart was severely damaged. He predicted that Alexander had two weeks to live. When the doctor told me there was no way to save Alexander, and that it would be easier for me if Alexander were hospitalized, I refused his advice. At this point, my role as caretaker officially began.

Knowing that Alexander was mortally ill and being alone with this knowledge toughened me up. Because I wanted to be a comfort, not the source of an argument, I went along with Alexander's belief that it was the flu, a minor illness—just a temporary weakened state.

While it was a privilege to be present with Alexander for the short time that was left, it was also difficult to witness his desire to stay and work when it was clear that his time was over. We didn't talk very much. Our connection had always been nonverbal anyway. We were communicating differently as his needs changed, and I, young and malleable as I was, became adept at finding new ways to attach and stay connected. They were visceral. Knowing him well enough to anticipate his needs, I felt his hunger and knew instinctively when he was thirsty or needed a window opened. My visible but silent presence comforted both of us.

During those final two weeks of his life at home with me, he retained his dignity, never succumbing to the panic of pain or loss of physical strength. He acted with the maturity and acceptance of a life well-conceived and experienced. This part of the story— being alone with him when he died, accompanying him and protecting him for the brief time he was experiencing physical fragility—was an important part of my knowing him and of accessing a certain part of myself.

Alexander Archipenko died on February 25, 1964, in bed at our home. When he gasped for air, it sounded like a baby's first cry. Then he was gone. While our parting was not unexpected, it was shocking. It seemed too abrupt. I surprise myself writing about it this way, since I never described the actual experience to anyone. It felt extremely intimate being present and truly alone with a death. It was daunting. However, I wasn't able to cry. Instead, I remember feeling very rigid.

The doctor had explained that, because he was at home, I most probably would be alone with him when he died and would need to immediately make phone calls and take charge. That's what happened. I called the doctor, who must have called the police. They were the first to arrive. I'm not sure who called the undertaker. Much to my surprise, the police asked questions as though it were a crime scene—all rather callous, but necessary. The undertaker came next while I was away from the bedroom being distracted by the police. I could hear the undertaker making metallic sounds. It was abusive to have all those strangers there, rattling around and being official. By the time my parents arrived, Alexander had been taken away.

Recalling that day and the first night without him brings me back to a time which I'd emotionally buried for many years in a fitful way. My mother stayed in the house that first night and slept with me in the double bed which Alexander and I had shared. She said I woke her in the middle of the night when I wrapped my legs around hers.

I was still unable to cry at the funeral, an event where I was feeling many more emotions than just sadness.

* * *

Archipenko's funeral at the Frank E. Campbell Funeral Home on Madison Avenue felt like two separate services at the same time. There was a schism as sharp as death itself, both social and emotional. The formality of the elaborate funeral at Campbell's was partially engineered by the Ukrainian community, who arranged for a Ukrainian chorus, full and ruthlessly religious in tone, to echo in the large chapel. Archipenko's funeral was a major event in the New York Ukrainian community, and the Ukrainian mourners arrived en masse. They were intent on claiming Archipenko as a national hero of the country he'd enthusiastically left in his youth and to which he never expected or wanted to return. It was as if they were at his funeral to reclaim him as a hero for their diaspora.

Disturbed because I requested a closed casket and refused to include the death mask and statuary which were conventions in a Greek Orthodox service, the Ukrainians made it clear in their manner and clustering that they existed in a parallel universe which they were intent upon maintaining.

I was too uncomfortable and exhausted to accommodate anybody but myself. I needed to survive this part of the ordeal as simply as possible. Alexander had only too recently mourned Angelica's death with all the conventions of his culture. He felt her loss deeply and was perhaps helped by the support of rituals which engaged social support. But I was of another generation and cultural history, with different traditions. My Jewish background, although casual, still sounded its edict against idol worship and may have been the strongest unconscious influence for my funeral choice for Alexander. While I was aware that Alexander would probably have chosen an open casket with memento photographs, rituals of death such as open caskets, incense, death masks, embalming, and sarcophaguses all felt excessively morbid and too public to me. What was distasteful for me was an essential part of the cycle for a Christian of Greek Orthodox heritage.

Furthermore, Edward Fry, the ambitious young art historian whom I asked to give the eulogy, didn't emphasize the importance of Alexander's Ukrainian background or religious upbringing, but spoke instead as an awestruck academician, addressing an audience who was invisible to the Ukrainian community. Fry had befriended Alexander when we were in Paris and, for his scholarly research, spent a considerable amount of time interviewing him in Paris and later in New York about the Cubist years.

The Ukrainians who attended the funeral, and there were many, grouped together in another reception room away from me. My mother stayed close by me, all her maternal instincts in place, and I tried to surround myself with the familiar faces of family and friends. However, also in attendance were many people I didn't know. As the Ukrainian chorus sang, one very hysterical woman, whom nobody seemed to know, had to be removed from the room. By the time the ceremony was over, the anemones on Alexander's coffin had wilted.

I also contributed a disturbance. The Ukrainian mourners were upset when I declined to order and pay for a fleet of limousines for their transport to Woodlawn Cemetery. Fortunately, the funeral home asked my permission first before they sent out the order. However, it was quite different with the exorbitant bill for the Ukrainian chorus, which I hadn't ordered. At the time I was irritated by their attitude of entitlement and didn't understand their behavior as respect for Alexander.

The burial was as Alexander had planned—next to his first wife, marked by his bronze enlargement of the sculpture Angelica had realized after her stroke.

Maruska Sumyk, who, with her husband, had been friends with me before and during my marriage to Alexander, now diverted all the Ukrainian mourners to her home and may have encouraged the belief that Alexander planned to give his Woodstock property, as well as his sculptures, to the Ukrainian Academy of Arts and Sciences in the United States. Maruska and her husband never spoke to me again. It was clear that while Alexander was alive, the closeness of their relationship with him, and thus their position in Ukrainian society, had hinged on their positive and kind behavior toward me. Emotionally, I was at the breaking point. I felt that I came from the wrong tribe. When members of the Ukrainian community ultimately questioned the legitimacy of my marriage, accompanied by a claim that Archipenko's work had been promised to the Ukrainian Academy of Arts and Sciences, the schism was complete.

Meanwhile, I had a more immediate problem. With my mother—who insisted on coming—as my companion, I set up an appointment with Herr Stangl in Munich. Just two weeks after the funeral, I was on a flight to Germany.

* * *

My mother and I both dressed carefully for the occasion, choosing smart suits in dark colors, good gloves and shoes, and handbags neither too small nor too large. Our ladylike appearance belied our goal and our strategy. A major exhibition of sculptures and drawings at Galerie Stangl had opened just a few days before Alexander died, and upon the news of his death, collectors had immediately reserved work. Before we arrived, I had sent word that all sales were to be suspended.

What Stangl didn't know was that of the twenty-three drawings in the show, at least eleven were falsely dated on purpose by Alexander. But I knew. I wanted those drawings off the market, and I took charge. Alexander's life and death have given me a strong and abiding determination that has never wavered. And at that time, I needed all my resources.

Galerie Stangl was completely filled with Archipenko sculptures and drawings. I barely had a chance to look at the installation before my mother and I were corralled into a large office that doubled as a private viewing room. It was all done in beige, pristine to the point of being clinical.

We'd decided beforehand that if Stangl had a lawyer present, we would walk out and go to the American embassy for help finding an American lawyer who knew German and international law. I had to be sure that the "early" drawings were removed, put away, and explained later. And a new contract had to be created, one which could be enforced. Seated at a medium-sized white oval conference table along with Stangl was a woman I assumed to be a secretary, and a gentleman who was introduced as a lawyer. I glanced at my mother. We'd had no real hope of a casual meeting, but this was beginning to feel potentially hostile.

After the initial introductions, I asked Mr. Stangl whether he would honor my request for a current statement of sales, an adjustment of prices, and a new contract. He had the demeanor of a serious, precise person. Under other circumstances, I probably would have gotten along with him.

As I spoke, he flared up and became almost disoriented. At that point, the woman whom I had assumed to be his secretary discreetly introduced herself as his wife and asked me to help her calm him down. She explained that he still suffered from an old war injury which affected his emotional control—a brain injury that had never totally healed and still jeopardized his health.

At this point my mother, who hadn't said a word, gave me a little kick under the table, probably to reassure me that she was at my side. In this overly-charged atmosphere, I stood up and announced, "I would like to end the meeting and will continue it after I've consulted with a local attorney." By the next day we had engaged an international lawyer recommended by the American embassy.

Stangl stayed away from the negotiations, which were conducted by the two lawyers until they met with my satisfaction. In the end, the exhibition was not taken down. Everything was settled so that the drawings were no longer for sale (only one had already been sold). Works that had already sold—or had been claimed for sale—remained at the original price, and other prices were raised. None of this wrangling would have been necessary if I'd been comfortable telling Stangl about the problematic drawings.

I left Germany feeling confident that I was capable of damage control and could meet the challenge of other unfinished business when I returned to New York. Because Alexander died before he could move in to his new building in Chelsea, work remained in the old loft—as in a temporary tomb—waiting to be inventoried, appraised, and then moved.

As an artist's widow, the protector of an important legacy, I also needed to understand the ever-changing art world, which seemed to be hidden in a thick jungle with much of its activity invisible to me. My sense of isolation was overwhelming. There was much to sort out, and little reliable guidance.

* * *

The cold windy air on Madison Avenue swept me up the front steps for my first meeting with Klaus Perls after Alexander's funeral. There were two things on my mind: I wanted to have a memorial exhibition for Alexander, and I needed to make some immediate sales to take care of estate taxes. Perls was my go-to person to meet both of those goals.

Dolly was sitting at the desk in the rear gallery. Standing up as she greeted me, her face reflected as much empathy as she could dish up. She signaled Klaus that I'd arrived. With a paternal smile he approached and then offered his hand to shake. It was going to be all business.

The tiny elevator took us to private quarters on the next floor. Perls had never invited Alexander to this floor—for either business or pleasure. Here was the private showroom where clients viewed individual works, with the Perls's private collection of Benin bronzes in the background. The room was neutral, quiet, and very beige, locked into an upper middle-class sensibility. The muffled sounds of Upper East Side traffic gently seeped in.

Maintaining his natural formality, Perls inquired how I was doing. I replied that I was well and hoped he was planning a memorial exhibition to honor Alexander. Instead of just saying "no," he insulted both Alexander and me by agreeing to a show if I would pay for the catalogue.

I didn't even reply. However, I was not intimidated as he brought up the next subject. He was interested in buying specific works. I made my deal. With that check and the Stangl sales, I would be able to clear the estate taxes. Although I maintained a superficially cordial relationship with Klaus and Dolly, I knew as I rode back down the elevator that I would never choose to show Alexander's work at the Perls Galleries again.

As Alexander's widow, I had to pick up where he left off, maintaining financial stability in order to protect his artistic legacy. To that end, I dealt with gallerists, historians, critics, and the full cast of art world personalities from whom Alexander had previously protected me. At twenty-eight years old, I was learning I could be clearheaded and tough. I did the sensible thing and sold our house in the West Village. As I focused on settling the estate, selling property, and consolidating Alexander's interests with mine, for the most part I was up to the task, but the toll was heavy. Today, after having raised four children on my own, I realize it was probably fortunate that I didn't have the added complication of raising a child while I was newly widowed and settling his estate—which would take another two years.

Emotionally, however, I remained frozen. Three weeks after Alexander's funeral, I realized that my jaw ached. I'd still been unable to cry and it would be a full year before I could.

While Alexander was alive and his presence was pervasive, it had never entered my mind that I would miss him. Now my attachment to him not only remained, but became more intense. During that first year, he frequently appeared to me in my dreams. When I was finally able to weep, a year after his death, it was only in state of deep meditation. Then I could cry in a way which was calm and refreshing, the tears streaming without sobs or emotional distress. Eventually, I began to move from a feeling of abandonment to one of independence and freedom. Alexander still felt close, but only when I needed him present—not all the time as an ache.

When I'd sculpted Alexander's portrait before he became ill, it had been very relaxing—almost like knitting a scarf without instructions—because I had to do it from memory. Although he was game, he was in constant motion and had no intention of sitting for the portrait. Working in three dimensions is very different than drawing or painting. It's not an illusion you produce, although it could fall into the category of an expression. But I knew what I was doing. Familiarity was soothing. It was a simple task of moving the clay until I found his image. His portrait in clay was a map with shifts in terrain. Wrinkles? No, just the pull of gravity which loosens the muscles' grip on youth.

When I knew he was dying, it never entered my mind that my life would continue to be about him after his death.

It has.

Epilogue
Fifty Years Later

Eventually I gave birth to four children, each with a different father, but I never remarried. I believed it would be less complicated to raise my children as a single parent. At times it was even entertaining to exhibit my social contrariness to a world which was unprepared for out-of-wedlock children unless they came from an underprivileged background. Once again, I disappointed my family by breaking a social pattern.

My personal life was always in flux, but this seemed natural to my temperament. I was the token unwed mother at Upper East Side social events of the seventies. Although my eccentric social behavior was now embedded, discretion was second nature to such a degree that only recently, I was surprised to learn from an old New York neighbor and friend that she and the other mothers in my building had always assumed I was a pioneer example of a family created through artificial insemination.

What was it like to be a very young woman married to a seventy-year-old man who defined himself in this seemingly eccentric yet profound way? That question became a major theme in my life. Initially it disturbed my family, and it remains part of the puzzle that my four children, who are not his but who share his legacy, would like to unravel.

Dignity, nobility, sensuality, and his final perceptions about creativity were only part of the mix. If in his final years he was obtuse about networking and commerce, that story needs to be told in the context of his tenaciousness. I saw that fame was a curse which most people defined as good luck. Having it and losing it—the constant struggle to be on the top of the pile—could enervate one's sight and funnel perception. Alexander experienced that in his lifetime, and I witnessed his final swan song. That melody has haunted me for fifty years.

The years I spent with Alexander so long ago have still not turned to ash. For in essence, I've always remained married to him: his "being" remains in the work that he left behind, and I remain its guardian. This role has given coherence, structure, and stability, as well as longevity, to my working life. In the year 2000, I founded the Archipenko Foundation, with my children—Alexander, David, Andrew, and Anna Gray—comprising the board. It's housed in Woodstock, in the original structure that was the Archipenko Art School. Working together with a small, dedicated staff, we plan to launch an online catalogue raisonné of Alexander's sculptures. The Archipenko Foundation recently digitalized much of the documentation which was earlier donated to the Archives of American Art, and much of the archival material which refreshed my memory for this book will be made accessible online as well. In recent years, the major auction houses, museums, and dealers have done due diligence with Archipenko by relying on the expertise supported by the documentation at the Archipenko Foundation.

As I have matured, after briefly navigating my own career as a visual artist, the steady force and the anchor of my being has been my experience of Alexander. When my only husband's life ended, my life continued to move on so that now, at seventy-eight years old myself, the review of my past with Alexander Archipenko has even more meaning for me.

I live on the property that was the Archipenko Summer Art School. It is here that I had the joy of being a student, a wife, an artist, and an adult raising a family. The walk to the waterfall remains; some trees have fallen and some have grown, rocks have shifted, but the moss prevails.

Although Alexander died in 1964, for me, his presence continues in his art. The history of his work and its documentation, presentation, and preservation has occupied my attention for the last fifty years. What I have discovered as I study the work is that my perception of it keeps changing. It has its own vitality.

Perhaps great art is the true "Fountain of Youth"—first for the artist and then for the perpetual viewer.

Frances Archipenko Gray with her poodle, Lucy, in Bearsville, NY, May 2014

Notes

Chapter Two

1. This dialogue was inspired by an interview with Angelica Archipenko which is preserved at the Alexander Archipenko papers, 1904–1986 (bulk 1930–1964), Archives of American Art, Smithsonian Institution, cited from here on as Archipenko papers. The date of the interview is unknown, circa 1955–57. A digitized version is available at the Archipenko Foundation, S09-item2_pp.1-11.
2. Katherine Jánszky Michaelsen, "Alexander Archipenko, 1887–1964," in Katherine Jánszky Michaelsen and Nehama Guralnik, *Alexander Archipenko: A Centennial Tribute* (Washington: National Gallery of Art, 1986), pp. 75–79.
3. Archipenko papers, digitized version, S02-1936-item14_p.11.
4. Michaelsen, "Alexander Archipenko," p. 76.
5. Ibid.
6. Ibid., p. 79.
7. Archipenko papers, letter from Archipenko to Alfred Barr, dated December 22, 1943.

Chapter Four

1. Archipenko papers, letter from Archipenko to Klihm, dated September 15, 1955, S02-correspondence_1955_Item00033.
2. Ibid.

Chapter Five

1. Howard Devree, "About Art and Artists: Whitney Museum and National Academy offer Representative Group Shows" *The New York Times*, November 14, 1956, L 49.
2. Archipenko papers, digitized version, S02-1956-item34_p.448 (December 5, 1956).
3. Ibid., S02-1957-item35_p.16 (February 6, 1957).

Chapter Six

1. Stuart Preston, "Diverse Sculpture and Painting," *The New York Times*, October 20, 1957, X13.
2. Robert Coates, "The Art Galleries," *The New Yorker*, November 2, 1957, p. 182.
3. Emily Genauer, "New Archipenko," *The Herald Tribune*, October 20, 1957, pagination unknown.
4. Robert Rosenblum, "Notes on Cleopatra," in *Archipenko: Drawings, Reliefs, and Constructions*, ed. Joan Marter (Bard College, Edith C. Blum Art Institute, 1984), pp. 9–10.

Chapter Seven

1. Archipenko papers, digitized version, S02-1958-item36_pp.163-164 (May 12, 1958).

Chapter Eight

1. Archipenko papers, digitized version, S02-1958-item36_pp.314-342.
2. Ibid., S02-1958-item36_p.344.
3. Archipenko Archives, folder for *Geometric Statuette*, correspondence (December 20, 1958).
4. Archipenko Archives, folder for *Geometric Statuette*, correspondence (January 19, 1959).
5. Archipenko Papers, digitized version, S02-1959-item37_pp.11-12 (January 20, 1959).

Chapter Nine

1. Archipenko papers, digitized version, S02-1959-item37_p.133 (June 9, 1959).
2. Ibid., S02-1959-item37_p.180 (July 7, 1959).
3. Ibid., S02-1959-item37_p.221 (August 12, 1959).
4. Michaelsen, "Alexander Archipenko," p. 83.
5. Ibid.

Chapter Ten

1. This letter, as well as the following quoted letters, is preserved at the Archipenko Foundation.
2. Archipenko papers, digitized version, S02-1960-item38_p.458 (October 17, 1960).
3. Ibid., S02-1960-item38_p.405 (September 26, 1960).

Chapter Eleven

1. Ibid., S02-1961-item39_pp.248-502 (May 15, 1961).
2. Sidney Geist, "Archipenko," *Arts Magazine*, vol. 35, no. 10 (September 1961), p. 71.

Chapter Twelve

1. "New Day for Old Cubist, Archipenko has a Comeback," *Life, European Edition*, March 26, 1962, pp. 79–80.
2. "Archipenko at 74," *Time*, January 5, 1962, no. 1, vol. LXXXIX, pp. 36–37.
3. Perls Galleries records, 1937–1997, Archives of American Art, Smithsonian Institution, letter dated May 18, 1961.
4. Archipenko Archives, folder for *Geometric Statuette*, correspondence (June 11, 1963).
5. Archipenko papers, digitized version, S02-1961-item39_p.41 (January 13, 1961).
6. Archipenko papers, digitized version, S02-1962-item40_p.700 (December 14, 1962), translated from German.

Biography: Alexander Archipenko

1887	Alexander Archipenko is born on May 30 in Kiev, Ukraine.
1902–05	Studies painting and sculpture at the Kiev Art School.
1906	Moves to Moscow, where he exhibits in group shows.
1909	Moves to Paris. Establishes studio at Montparnasse; associates with the artists' colony La Ruche.
1910	First public exhibition in Paris at the Salon des Indépendants XXVI, along with leading representatives of Cubism.
1911	Exhibits at the Salon d'Automne IX for the first time.
1912	Opens art school in Paris. Exhibits as member of Section d'Or at the Galerie la Boétie.
1913	Takes part in Armory Show in New York. First solo show in Berlin, at Herwarth Walden's Galerie Der Sturm.
1914	Participates in exhibition at the Mánes Fine Arts Association in Prague, with Brancusi and Duchamp-Villon. Futurists invite him to participate at the Esposizione Libera Futurista Internazionale in Rome. Creates first sculpto-paintings.
1914–18	Spends the war years in Cimiez, near Nice.
1918	Creates *Vase Woman I*.
1919	Exhibition tour through Europe starts in Geneva and runs through 1921; traveling locations include Zurich, Paris, London, Amsterdam, Brussels, Dresden, Munich, Düsseldorf, and New York.

1920	Solo show at Venice Biennale, Russian Pavilion.
1921	Moves to Berlin. Opens art school there while also keeping his studio in Paris. Marries Angelica Schmitz, a German sculptor who exhibits under the name Gela Forster. First solo show in the USA at the Société Anonyme, New York.
1923	Angelica and Alexander Archipenko move to the USA. Opens art school in New York.
1924	Solo exhibition at Kingore Gallery, New York, under the auspices of the Société Anonyme. Teaches summer art school in Woodstock, New York.
1929	Purchases thirteen acres of land on a rock quarry site in Bearsville, near Woodstock, New York. Becomes an American citizen. Establishes "Arko," a school of ceramics in New York City.
1932	Lectures on creativity at universities and colleges on the Pacific Coast, in the Midwest, and on the East Coast.
1933	Solo exhibition, Ukrainian Pavilion at Chicago World's Fair, "A Century of Progress." Presents forty-four works, including the *Mâ* series for the first time.
1935	Moves to Los Angeles; opens art school in Hollywood.
1936	Participates in *Cubism and Abstract Art* exhibition at the Museum of Modern Art, curated by Alfred Barr. Presents six sculptures: *Hero, Walking Woman, Boxing, Statuette, Bather, Woman Combing Her Hair.*
1937	Moves to Chicago. Invited by László Moholy-Nagy to teach at the New Bauhaus. In Germany, works by Archipenko are confiscated by the Nazis as "degenerate art."

1938	Opens "Modern School of Fine Arts and Practical Design" in Chicago. Opens summer art school on his own land in Bearsville, near Woodstock, New York.
1946–47	Returns to Chicago, teaches at the Institute of Design (formerly Bauhaus).
1949	Solo show in Berlin (Archipenko's first European exhibition after World War II).
1951	Teaches at Carmel Art Institute, California, University of Washington, Seattle, and University of Delaware.
1954	Retrospective *110th Exhibition, Fifty Years Production*, at Associated American Artists Galleries, New York.
1955	First large retrospective after World War II opens in Germany, traveling to several institutions, including Hessisches Landesmuseum Darmstadt, Städtische Kunsthalle Mannheim, and Städtische Kunstsammlungen Düsseldorf.
1956	Takes part in the Annual Exhibition at the Whitney Museum in New York City. Teaches at the University of British Columbia, Vancouver, Canada. Exhibits at Indiana State Teachers College, Pennsylvania.
1957	Shows recent polychrome sculptures and sculpto-paintings at Perls Galleries, New York City, and again takes part in the Annual Exhibition at the Whitney Museum. His wife Angelica dies on December 5.
1958	First collaboration with Eric Estorick of Grosvenor Gallery, London.
1959	Solo exhibition at Perls Galleries in New York City.
1960	Publishes his book *Archipenko: Fifty Creative Years, 1908–58*. Marries Frances Gray, an artist and former student, on August 1.

A large retrospective is opened in Germany, traveling to several institutions, including Karl Ernst Osthaus Museum in Hagen and Saarländisches Landesmuseum Saarbrücken.
Several of Archipenko's early plasters, which had been stored with friends near Cannes since 1921, are returned to him.

1961   Solo exhibition at Grosvenor Gallery in London.

1962   Solo exhibition at Perls Galleries, New York City.
A retrospective of Archipenko's work takes place at the Winnipeg Art Gallery, Winnipeg, Canada.
An exhibition dedicated to Archipenko's work on paper opens at Saarländisches Landesmuseum Saarbrücken, also traveling to other venues in Germany.
Solo exhibition at Galerie Im Erker in St. Gallen, Switzerland.

1963   Creates the portfolio *Les Formes Vivantes*, a series of ten lithographs in an edition of seventy-five, with Erker-Presse in St. Gallen, Switzerland.
In April, a solo exhibition opens at the Palazzo Barberini in Rome, traveling to Milan in the fall.

1964   Solo exhibition at Galerie Stangl in Munich opens on February 14.
Alexander Archipenko dies on February 25 in New York City.

Acknowledgments

Much appreciation to my writing coach and personal editor, Susan Brown, without whom this memoir would have remained an endless struggle rather than a pleasurable effort. Thank you to my agent, Barbara Braun, who believed in the book and brought it to Hirmer. I also extend my thanks to the staff at the Archipenko Foundation: Alexandra Keiser for her fact-checking, Chris Hyde for his image preparation, and Pierrette Kim for her patience with my preoccupation. Not to be forgotten is the team at Hirmer, Rainer Arnold, Jutta Allekotte, and Katja Durchholz, for their positive feedback and timely organization. Working directly with Rita Forbes, who did the final editing, assured me that all the rough edges of my writing were smoothed out.

Picture credits

Chapter, epilogue, and cover photographs

Archipenko Archives, The Archipenko Foundation, Bearsville, NY: pp. 6, 22, 36, 50, 64, 76, 100, 112, 118, 130, 144, 166, 180, front cover, frontispiece, back cover.

Personal collection of Frances Gray, photography by Kathleen Ruiz: epilogue.

Figures

Archipenko Archives, The Archipenko Foundation, Bearsville, NY: 1, 3, 7, 8, 10, 18, 19, 20, 22, 27, 35, 36, 43, 50, 51, 67.

The Archipenko Foundation, Bearsville, NY, photography by Erma Estwick: 2, 24, 49, 62, 63.

The Archipenko Foundation, Bearsville, NY, photography by Chip Porter: 23, 26, 57, 58, 59, 60, 61, 68.

The Archipenko Foundation, Bearsville, NY, photography by Jeffrey Sturges: 6, 21, 28, 29, 31, 34, 37, 41, 42, 47, 48, 54, 64.

Courtesy of Art Gallery of Hamilton, Ontario, Canada: 45.

Photo © Christie's Images / Bridgeman Images: 39.

Courtesy of Galerie Thomas, Munich, photography by Erma Estwick: 40.

Personal collection of Frances Gray: 13, 14, 15, 16, 32, 33.

Peggy Guggenheim Collection, Venice (Solomon R. Guggenheim Foundation, NY): 11.

The Solomon R. Guggenheim Foundation / Art Resource, NY, photography by Kristopher McKay: 12.

Hirshhorn Museum and Sculpture Garden, Smithsonian Institution, Washington, DC. Gift of Joseph H. Hirshhorn, 1972. Photography by Lee Stalsworth: 5.

Courtesy of Lynden Sculpture Garden, Milwaukee, WI, photography by Claire Ruzicka: 56.

The Museum of Fine Arts, Houston, TX. Museum purchase funded by the Board of Governors of Rice University in grateful memory of Alice Pratt Brown: 46.

Digital image © The Museum of Modern Art / Licensed by SCALA / Art Resource, NY: 52, 69.

Norton Simon Museum, gift of Harold P. and Jane F. Ullman to the Blue Four Galka Scheyer Collection: 4.

Saarlandmuseum, Saarbrücken, photography by Tom Gundelwein: 55, 65.

Photo © Sheldon Museum of Art: 9.

Smithsonian American Art Museum, Washington, DC / Art Resource, NY: 66.

Courtesy of Sotheby's, New York: 38.

Collection of the Tel Aviv Museum of Art. Gift of the Goeritz Family, London, 1956, in memory of Erich Goeritz. Photography by Elad Sarig: 44.

By Petro Hrycyk for The Ukrainian Museum in New York for the exhibition catalogue *Alexander Archipenko: Vision and Continuity*, published in 2005: 17, 25, 30, 53.

Captions for chapter images

Chapter One: Archipenko in his New York studio, 1960

Chapter Two: Angelica and Dr. Wolodymyr Wozniak at Archipenko's seventieth birthday party at the Ukrainian Institute, May 1957

Chapter Three: Archipenko at his seventieth birthday party at the Ukrainian Institute, May 1957

Chapter Four: Archipenko at work in his studio on Dignity, 1960

Chapter Five: Frances Gray in her studio, circa 1957–58

Chapter Six: Frances Gray, Lincoln Arcade Building, circa 1957–58

Chapter Seven: Archipenko with Sappho, 1963

Chapter Eight: Archipenko and Frances Gray, Saarbrücken, 1960

Chapter Nine: Archipenko and Frances Gray at the Saarbrücken vernissage with Walking in background, 1960

Chapter Ten: Archipenko and Frances Gray, St. Gallen, 1963

Chapter Eleven: Archipenko and Frances Gray with Dr. Erich Wiese, Darmstadt, circa 1960s

Chapter Twelve: Archipenko at the Saarbrücken vernissage, 1960

Chapter Thirteen: Archipenko (right) with unnamed dignitaries, Rome exhibition, 1963

Published by
Hirmer Verlag GmbH
Nymphenburgerstr. 84
80636 Munich
Germany

Project management
Jutta Allekotte, Rainer Arnold, Katja Durchholz

Copyediting
Rita Forbes, Munich

Digital image and rights project manager
Christopher Hyde

Graphic design, typesetting, and production
Katja Durchholz

Pre-press and repro
Reproline mediateam GmbH, Munich

Paper
LuxoArt samt new, 150 g/qm

Typefaces
Bk Avenir Book, Bauer Bodoni

Printing and binding
Passavia Druckservice, Passau

Printed in Germany

Bibliographical data of the Deutsche Nationalbibliothek:
The Deutsche Nationalbibliothek lists this publication
in the Deutsche Nationalbibliografie;
detailed bibliographic information is available
on the Internet at http://www.dnb.de.

ISBN 978-3-7774-2248-0
www.hirmerpublishers.com

Frontispiece
Alexander Archipenko at the Saarbrücken vernissage, 1960